Paint me black

Memories of Croker Island and other journeys

Claire Henty-Gebert

Aboriginal Studies Press

First published in 2005
Aboriginal Studies Press for the
Australian Institute of Aboriginal
and Torres Strait Islander Studies
GPO Box 553, Canberra, ACT 2601

The views expressed in the publication
are those of the author and not necessarily
those of the Australian Institute of Aboriginal
and Torres Strait Islander Studies.

National Library of Australia Cataloguing-In-
Publication data:

Henty-Gebert, Claire, 1930– .
Paint me black

ISBN 0 85575 399 4.

1. Henty-Gebert, Claire, 1930– . 2. Aborigines,
Australian — Northern Territory. 3. Northern
Territory — Antiquities. 4. Northern Territory
— History. 5. Frew River Region (N.T.) —
History. I. Title

Printed by National Captial Printing
Design and typesetting by Rachel Ippoliti,
Aboriginal Studies Press

This project has been assisted by
the Australian Government
through the Australia Council, its
arts funding and advisory body.

Contents

Preface

Peter Forrest

Claire Henty-Gebert has lived a remarkable life, through times and circumstances well outside the personal experience of most Australians. This introduction aims to provide a framework to help all Australians better understand Claire's life story.

Claire's story is an inspiring one, told in simple, direct and powerful language. Despite misfortune and discrimination, Claire has always remained confident that things would turn out for the best, and she has been generous in her assessment of the role played by the people who have had an impact on her life.

The story has necessarily been pieced together from conventional documentary sources, and from people's memories. We can be grateful that Claire, and those around her, have clung so very jealously to their personal stories, allowing us to benefit from what might have been forgotten.

*

Claire was born near Frew River station, the child of white settler Harry Henty and Ruby Ngwarie, an Alyawarra Aboriginal woman.

Frew River is located about 200km southeast of Tennant Creek, and about 400km north-northeast of Alice Springs. Harry Henty was one of a small group of white settlers struggling for a toehold in the region in the 1920s. Ruby was one of a number of Aboriginal people who 'came in' to the camps of the whites on the promise of a better standard of living than their traditional situation provided, in return for labour, tobacco and sexual services.

The Frew River region was then literally one of Australia's last frontiers, one of the last places where white settlers and Aborigines met for the first time. It is an ancient and interesting landscape, ranging from sand plains and spinifex ridges to watercourses cutting through mountain ranges. Occasional large permanent waterholes are a surprising feature of what is otherwise an arid land.

As a mirror of the physical landscape, the region is also full of historical interest. It is the country of the Kaytetye and Alyawarra Aboriginal people.

John McDouall Stuart was the first white man to traverse the region, during his 1860, 1861 and 1862 journeys from South Australia to the north coast. Stuart's final success resulted in the creation of the Northern Territory in 1863, and in 1870, the commencement of the Overland Telegraph Line's construction.

The telegraph line was the catalyst for the first permanent white settlement in the region when the Barrow Creek telegraph station was built in 1872. On 23 February 1874 it was the scene of an attack by Kaytetye Aboriginals. Telegraph employees Stapleton and Franks were fatally speared. Punitive expeditions followed which imposed savage reprisals and decimated the Kaytetye.

In late 1873, Mounted Police Troopers had been appointed to the telegraph stations at Charlotte Waters and Barrow Creek, and Mounted Constable Samuel Gason was on his way to Barrow Creek when the Kaytetye attack occurred. Gason immediately summoned colleagues from Charlotte Waters and The Peake (in South Australia) and over the next few months they rode across the surrounding country, killing dozens, perhaps hundreds, of Aborigines — whether or not they had any connection with the Barrow Creek attack.

For the next half century, relationships between local Aborigines and white settlers were uneasy, and often marked by violence.

Regional pastoral settlement began in 1884 when the Barrow Creek Pastoral Company stocked the country now known as Stirling and Murray Downs. Four years later, in 1888, the South Australian-based Willowie Land and Pastoral Company stocked Frew River and Elkedra stations, and took over the Barrow Creek Pastoral Company enterprise.

Due mainly to sustained Aboriginal resistance to the pastoral intrusion, these stations were abandoned from 1896. Huge sums of money were lost by the early pastoralists who abandoned the country without even bothering to muster the cattle. The cattle ran wild until after 1910, when a second generation of would-be pastoralists saw an opportunity.

Prior to the turn of the century there had been interest in the mineral potential of the area with wolfram discovered in 1898. However, wolfram had little commercial value until the outbreak of World War One, when its price skyrocketed. Wolfram then became strongly sought after for use in the manufacture of hardened steels for armaments.

By 1915 several wolfram mining leases were being worked in the Hatches Creek and Frew River areas. The mineral was literally scratched from surface workings or from shallow shafts. There was little mechanisation, and a heavy reliance on Aboriginal labour in the mines. White miners and Aborigines lived in close proximity to one another, in a relationship of interdependence for food and labour.

Living conditions were extremely basic for both groups. The white miners' camps were little more than bough huts, with the occasional sheet of galvanised iron providing the only evidence of imported luxury. The Aborigines camped nearby. Meat and milk from goats were the most common foodstuffs, supplemented by flour, sugar and tea, and bush tucker.

The wolfram workings provided yet another means of subsistence for a group of white men who came into the area seeking an opportunity to begin cattle stations. Their strategy was to muster and brand the area's wild cattle, or, in more than one instance, to build a herd with animals stolen from established stations. These men were generally skilled in outback ways; experts in the working of cattle and Aboriginal labour. They had little or no capital, but their skills and willingness to live hard were an even more valuable resource.

They claimed areas of country around the good waterholes, and began to muster and subdue wild cattle. Gradually, they formed stations. They mustered cattle and turned them off to markets when demand justified it. At other times they focused their efforts on mining wolfram at Hatches Creek or Wauchope.

Typically, these men first came into the area to work on the telegraph line, or to mine wolfram. When they saw a more permanent opportunity they decided to stay.

Harry Henty was one such man; a telegraph linesman turned stockman, a small-scale pastoralist and miner. He was a sergeant in the 12th Battalion, and was recommended for the Military Medal for action in 1917 at Bullecourt. It seems that Henty worked first with Tom Hanlon, a lessee of Frew River station, and then took over the station from Hanlon, perhaps in association with another local identity, George Birchmore, of nearby Kurrundi station. By 1928 the station was described as being Henty's.

Henty was fatally shot in December 1928, during an affray with an Aboriginal man, Willaburta Jack.

This incident seems to have occurred when Henty left his Frew River station to go to the camp of miner George Masters, about 30 miles away. The Aboriginal man, Willaburta Jack, worked at Masters' camp. Henty was searching for his stock boys who had left Frew River some days before. An argument developed between Henty and Willaburta Jack, and Henty grabbed a rifle, which he loaded. Willaburta Jack retreated inside a hut.

Henty approached the hut. Witnesses said that they heard a shot from inside the hut, and saw Henty fall, with a wound to his head. One witness said, 'Henty would have shot Willaburta if the latter had not shot him first.'

The incident was an extraordinary one, for few Aboriginal people in that time and place were courageous (or foolhardy) enough to resist the commonplace acts of violence by white men. However, it seems that Willaburta Jack acted only after great provocation by Henty, a man who was known to be extremely violent and callous. A reading of the proceedings of Willaburta Jack's trial in Darwin indicates that almost everyone involved wanted to see him acquitted of a murder charge.

After the shooting, Willaburta Jack fled the scene with his wife, and remained at liberty until he was arrested by Constable Murray, at Curtis station, near Wauchope, in June 1929. Willaburta Jack was charged with murder, and tried in Darwin in July 1929. He was acquitted by the jury, which quickly returned a verdict of justifiable homicide. In those days, in cases where an Aboriginal person was the defendant, such verdicts invariably required very clear evidence in the defendant's favour.

The arresting officer, Constable Murray (responsible earlier in 1928 for the 'Coniston killings'), took Willaburta Jack back to the Barrow Creek area. On 11 September 1929, the Barrow Creek police were advised that Willaburta Jack had died at the Devils Marbles, his death due to a gunshot wound. Other reports say that he died as a result of poisoning. (For accounts of Henty's death, see M. Cartwright, *Territory Tales*, Alice Springs 1997; M. Cartwright *Missionaries, Aborigines & Welfare Settlement days in the NT*, Alice Springs 1996; V.E. Turner *The Good Fella Missus*,

Adelaide 1938; *Northern Standard* newspaper (Darwin) 2 August 1929).

Not everyone in the Frew River area was saddened by Henty's death. Henty was notoriously callous in his dealings with Aborigines. Old timer Walter Smith recalled, 'Harry Henty had a little block of land, and he had a few horses and cattle there. And he used to go and get all the native girls. Young girls, and take them over to his camp there. They was only kids and he used to cut them with a pocket knife and rape them.' (Walter Smith, cited in *Man From Arltunga*, R.G. Kimber, Hesperian 1986).

Given Henty's death in December 1928, and accepting the oral tradition that Harry Henty was in fact Claire's natural father, we can assume that Claire was born no later than about August 1929, although the exact date of her birth is not known.

The first clear historical evidence we have of young Claire comes from the Barrow Creek police journal of Monday 11 February 1935.

The journal entry records: 'Mr. E. Richards brought to stn. a half caste female child, aged about 6 years, and known as Clara Henty. She was sent in from Kurrundi by Mr. Birchmore at MC request.' (The abbreviation MC almost certainly refers to 'Mounted Constable'.) On 12 February the record reads: 'Half caste child being cared for at stn. pending suitable opportunity sending her to Alice Springs Bungalow.'

And on 14 February 'half caste child Clara Henty sent to Bungalow Alice Springs with Mr. Borlace' (spelling unclear in original).

The Bungalow was a government institution established in Alice Springs in 1914, when Police Sergeant Robert Stott provided emergency accommodation for Topsy Smith and her seven part-Aboriginal children. The family had come into town from Arltunga, following the death of Topsy Smith's husband, a white miner.

The place became an institution to which part-Aboriginal children were brought, either compulsorily after removal from their mothers, or voluntarily by guardians who wished the children to have some chance of an education.

Topsy Smith took charge of the institution at first, but in 1915 Mrs Ida Standley took over as matron. What began as a shelter soon became a government institution to receive and bring up children who had been brought in, pursuant to policies that part-Aboriginal children should be taken away from Aboriginal camps and trained for entry into white society.

In its first years the Bungalow was sited at the rear of the Stuart Arms Hotel, and provided for anything up to fifty children. There was constant criticism of its location in the town area, and in 1928 the institution was moved to Jay Creek, some 50 km from the town. Jay Creek was a poor site: water was scarce and there were other difficulties.

In late 1932 the institution was moved again, this time to the Alice Springs Telegraph Station, which had just been vacated by the Postmaster General's Department. By 1935 there were about one hundred and thirty children at the Bungalow.

In 1929, J.W. Bleakley, Chief Protector of Aboriginals in Queensland, delivered a report on the 'Aboriginal problem' in the Territory. In respect of part-Aboriginal children, Bleakley suggested that homes on island missions would be more suitable than government institutions.

Bleakley felt that the missions could offer separation from the corrupting influences of the towns, better conditions for the children, and lower costs. Implementation of these ideas was delayed until after 1940, but in that year it was officially decided that the missions should be given a bigger role in Aboriginal welfare.

It was resolved in Canberra that the government institutions for part-Aboriginal children at Darwin, Pine Creek, and Alice Springs should be closed down, and that all the children should be allocated to missions.

The Methodist Overseas Mission Board, which conducted missionary activity in the Northern Territory, resolved that a new Methodist mission, specifically for part-Aboriginal children, should be established, separate from any of the missions for Aborigines generally. In 1940 a site on Croker Island was selected by the Methodists.

In May 1941 the mission lugger *Larrpan* landed building materials and an advance party at Croker Island. Meanwhile, part-Aboriginal children in government care were selected for transfer to the various missions. In July 1941, sixty-eight children were moved from Pine Creek and Alice Springs to temporary quarters on Goulburn Island, pending the development of facilities on Croker Island.

By November 1941, four cottage homes on Croker Island were almost ready for occupation. On 25 November the *Larrpan* took forty-four children and four missionaries from Goulburn Island to Croker Island. More children and missionaries from Darwin soon arrived at Croker Island, and by December 1941 there were ninety-six children on the island.

It is clear from Claire's story that this was a happy time for the children. It is also overwhelmingly clear from Claire's own words, and from abundant additional evidence, that despite the harsh official policies, the missionaries on the island were full of compassion and practical concern for the children.

Just as the children were settling down on Croker Island, other civilians in the Territory's Top End were being ordered to evacuate their homes. The war against Japan had broken out on 8 December 1941 (Australian time), and an enemy attack on northern Australian was thought to be a matter of 'when, not if'. Within six weeks, most women and children and civilian men had been evacuated from Darwin.

However, at first no arrangements were made for the evacuation of the mission stations. It was not until 13 February 1942, six days before the first air raids on Darwin, that the missions were warned to plan for the evacuation of women and children.

By this time, the previously remote missions along the Arnhem Land coasts were right in the centre of a zone of great strategic significance and likely hostilities. From 1940, Advanced Operational Bases had been established around the north coasts of Australia, to create secure routes for the movement of aircraft across the north. The skies became busy with military aircraft.

Most white women and children on the coastal missions were evacuated in March 1942, but three women, Margaret Somerville, Olive Peake, and Jess March, chose to stay on Croker Island to help with the children. Finally, on 7 April 1942, the *Larrpan* arrived to collect everyone from Croker Island, for transport to the mainland.

It was the beginning of a remarkable exodus — by boat, on foot, by canoe, truck, and train. It ended ninety days later, in Sydney.

The Croker Island children spent the war years in and near Sydney. Again, they were happy years, at least for Claire, who undertook further schooling and acquired skills in crafts such as sewing.

A small group of boys returned to the island in July 1944, but the main body of children did not return until July 1946. There was indecision about returning the children to Croker Island, with one argument being that the children would have better futures in southern Australia. In the end, the children's own wishes prevailed. They shared the view that Croker Island was their home; it had been a happy home, and they wanted to go back to it as soon as possible. Throughout the war years, many girls had kept some of the island's sand which had been trapped in the hems of their skirts. 'Our beautiful island home' they said, as they touched the sand reassuringly.

The children resumed their lives on the island, grew up there, and, in some cases, like Claire, spent a good few years of their early adult lives on the island.

In 1967 the children's' cottages on Croker Island were closed. The last of the children were flown into Darwin, to begin residence in suburban homes (Somerville Homes, named after pioneer missionary Margaret Somerville) in Darwin.

The Methodist Church (Uniting Church in North Australia) adopted a policy of encouraging the former Croker Island children to seek out their families, to clarify their personal origins. Claire spent many years on her own quest for her identity.

She has now pieced the story together, and is content that her children and their descendants can now know their story.

Telling her life story brings together a history that, until relatively recently, was commonly swept under the carpet, and remained unknown to almost all Australians. We should be grateful to Claire for generously allowing all Australians to share in a story which tells us so much about our country's recent history.

Peter Forrest is a Darwin-based historian and writer.

Acknowledgements

First, I thank specially my daughters, Cyndia and Deanna, and my grand-daughter Isadora, for listening to hours of tape recordings, and typing up the first manuscript. Thank you to Peter and Sheila Forrest for helping to finalise the manuscript, research pictures and for writing the Preface. The photograph of the *Kalami* anchored at Belyuen, is courtesy of the Marjorie Harris Collection which is held by Peter and Sheila Forrest.

Thank you to the Australian Archives, Darwin; Anyinginyi Congress Aboriginal Co-operation, Tennant Creek; the Aboriginal Women Resource Centre, Winnellie; and the North Australian Aboriginal Legal Aid Service, Darwin. Thank you to Parks and Wildlife Commission of the Northern Territory in Alice Springs for finding the photo of my father standing in front of the Barrow Creek Telegraph Station.

Thank you to AIATSIS for providing a Research Grant which helped me with research, interviews and travel.

*

This research project was written especially for my family, my three daughters Cyndia Claire Henty-Roberts, Deanna Margaret Hodgins-Roberts and Wendy-Sue Patzwald; my nine grandchildren, Isadora Claire Roberts, Robert Shane Hodgins, Christian Allen Hodgins, Allen Ronald Hodgins, Candice Claire Pethybridge, Chrystal Claire Roberts, Csenta Claire Roberts, Sarah Claire Patzwald, Leroy John Patzwald;

and my great grandchildren, Jayden Robert Hodgins, Keinan William Pethybridge, Chynna Claire May Puckeridge, Jade Claire Joyce Devery, Tyson Lee Rundle, Raven Clara Russell, Kateea Clara Hodgins and Jason William Puckeridge (Jnr).

It is important for them to know who their ancestors were, to know what tribe they belong to on their maternal grandmother's side, and to have a sense of belonging to their country. I give this to them.

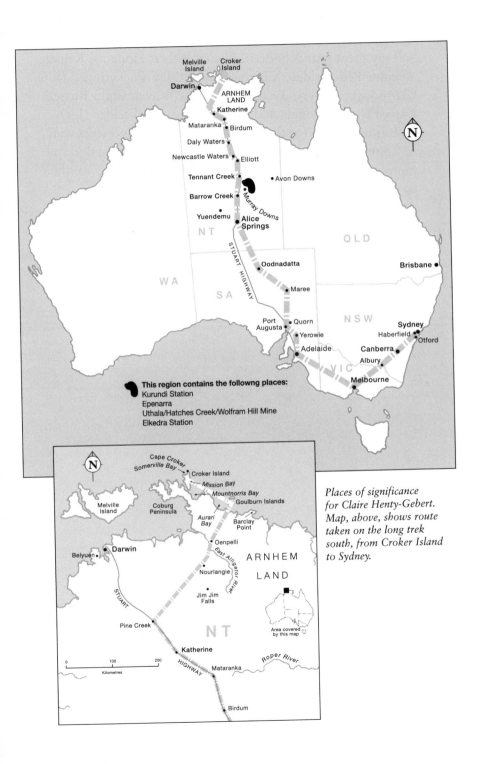

Places of significance
for Claire Henty-Gebert.
Map, above, shows route
taken on the long trek
south, from Croker Island
to Sydney.

Introduction

My name is Claire Henty-Gebert. I am one of the many thousands of children of Aboriginal descent who were separated from their Aboriginal mothers as a result of the government laws and policies in the Northern Territory during the 1900s. This story is based on my life-long search and dream of finding my mother, my siblings, my extended family, my birth place and country, my dreaming, and my sense of belonging.

I was born Clara Henty to my Aboriginal mother, Ruby, and a European pioneer telegraph linesman and later pastoralist, Harry Henty. This was at Hatches Creek in the Northern Territory, sometime during the 1920s. My birth certificate records 4 November 1930 as my birth date. However to this day the correct date of my birth remains unknown.

I believe that I must have been just a young child at the time of my separation because I have no memories either of my parents or my early childhood; just vivid memories of arriving at the Bungalow in Alice Springs. That's where I'll begin.

My skin brother, Murphy Japanangka, told me that I did not have an Aboriginal name at the beginning. I had only an English name from my 'daddy', Harry Henty, but that later my family called me Ngwarie. My tribe is Alyawarra and my dreaming is Kwatye which is 'rain'. My grandfather on my mother's side was a rainmaker. My family doesn't want his name mentioned, so I'll keep their wishes.

Another member of my extended family told me that I had a younger brother, who they still refer to as 'Dickie'. Murphy confirmed this information, saying that Dickie and I were the only children born to my parents. He also told me that my father was fatally shot by an Aboriginal man called Willaberta Jack, and that it was the death of my father that changed our lives forever.

Murphy remembers quite clearly the day I was taken away by Constable Croud. He recalls that I would have been about three or four years of age and that he and I were camped with our mothers and other children nearby at the Wolfram Hill Mine. He recalled that he was playing around the camp with his younger brother, Jimmy Dunno, while our mothers looked on. He said they didn't expect Constable Croud and the black trackers that day because up until then there'd been no policeman in the district. He described their coming, 'They just came from nowhere.'

There were Murphy's younger brothers NJ, and Jimmy Dunno, Dickie and I; all were taken by Constable Croud and the Aboriginal trackers.

This would be the last time that my family and I would see each other again, until some sixty odd years later.

European settlement

My two aunties, Jemima Napinjadi and Lena Dixon Nagala, told me that when the white settlers arrived on our country, the settlers forced our families off their land. The invasion of the settlers ended our way of life; the handing down and knowledge of hunting, dancing, gathering foods and bush medicines was no longer as it used to be.

My aunties remembered how their parents had told them of how as children their parents took them to the ceremonial waterholes and told them the stories that belonged to the waterholes and that country. They talked very fondly of significant places called 'Thuthuwa', 'Cupuda' and 'Uthala'.

They told how the settlers took control of the main waterholes and drove our people further and further from their traditional lands in search of food and water. The waterholes that were of no real use to the settlers were poisoned, so as to kill off as many Aboriginal people as they could.

My family said there were too many killings and too much bloodshed in those days. White stockmen on horseback would chase and shoot Aboriginal people at random. During the 1920s, many of our people fled to Bonney Well Station, owned then by Billy Curtis and now known as Greenwood Station. Others fled to Tennant Creek. Aunty Lena Nagala said that our people resisted the settlers' invasion at great lengths, but in the end they lost their land as well as their souls. Before long, many started drifting off their traditional lands to other areas. Lake Nash was one of them. She said that no one was safe in their own country anymore. The exodus to other neighbouring lands also caused fighting amongst the different groups of Aboriginal people.

Another major problem resulting in fighting and killings was that the pastoralists were stealing young Aboriginal girls from their families. Aboriginal men retaliated by killing the pastoralists' cattle and raiding the stations for food and supplies when they were left unprotected.

Eventually, one by one, in the 1880s, Murray Downs, Elkedra, Frew River and Kurundi Stations all closed down because of the loss of stock and stores. Later, the stockmen ran away because of their bosses' cruelty, and the distance and hardships in transporting cattle to buyers.

It wasn't until around 1919 that Bill Riley and Fred Kennedy re-established Elkedra Station. My father applied for various grazing licences surrounding Animbra Commonage in the mid-1920s. In 1927 he applied for and was granted various pastoral leases over the same lands, but shortly thereafter, on 15 December 1928, he was fatally shot by an Aboriginal man called Willaberta Jack.

There are many versions surrounding the circumstances of my father's death. I'm going to concentrate on the Aboriginal version as told to me by my relatives on my mother's side.

Aunty Jemima said that her brother Philomac and other Aboriginals worked for my father at Frew River. She remembers how her brother had been chained by the neck to a tree to prevent him from running way. Somehow he got free, and with some of the other Aboriginal workers, and still with the chain around his neck, he fled from Frew River to Hatches Creek. When Harry found that Philomac was missing he and Jack Spratt, a half-caste employee, followed Philomac and the other Aboriginal workers' tracks to a hut at Hatches Creek. This was owned by a Mr Masters, who my family said was well liked in the area. On their arrival, Harry told Jack Spratt that if anything should happen to him Jack was to leave as fast as he could to get help. It turned out that Mr Master was away at that time and had left his Aboriginal employee, Willaberta Jack, to look after things in his absence.

On their arrival, Harry asked Willaberta whether Philomac was there. Willaberta told him, 'No'; Philomac had come, but had since continued on his way. Harry didn't believe Willaberta and still insisted that Philomac was hiding in the hut. An argument erupted and shots were fired by both men at each other. A bullet from Harry's gun pierced Willaberta's shirt and grazed his skin, taking 'a bit of flesh', as described by my brother Murphy. Willaberta jumped on top of a table as Harry came through the doorway to the hut. The room was dark and Harry couldn't see properly. Willaberta then fired the fatal shot. Harry stumbled backwards several metres before collapsing to the ground.

My Aunty Lena said that my father was a very strong, tough man to have lasted on his feet as long as he did after he was shot. She said that Aboriginals from all over the country, as well as my extended family, worshipped Willaberta as a hero. They described him as a very clever, smart man who spoke and learnt well from the European settlers.

My father was buried on the banks of the Hatches Creek, opposite the spot where he had been shot.

They described Harry as a very cruel man to their people. Many did not show any remorse or sadness towards his death, except I guess my mother.

Willaberta hid from the police for several months before finally deciding to surrender himself to Billy Curtis at Greenwood Station. He was chained to a tree until the police arrived to escort him to Darwin. Willaberta was charged with the murder of my father and put on trial in Darwin, but he was found not guilty because there was insufficient evidence to convict him.

Some months after being released, Willaberta was found dead near Hatches Creek. My family have told me that he was poisoned while eating with his wife and one of the white miners at Arunjurra, an old mine, half way to Wauchope and east from Devils Marbles.

As the story goes, the miner insisted Willaberta and his wife eat dinner in his hut. When they sat down to eat, the miner pointed out to Willaberta's wife where he had placed her food on the table. He then pointed to the other plate of food, beckoning Willaberta to sit and eat. Willaberta became suspicious, thinking that he was being seated in a certain position to be shot, and after only a few mouthfuls of food beckoned his wife to leave with him.

He whispered into his wife's ear 'they might kill me'. Within minutes Willaberta fell to the ground dead — not far from where they had eaten. His wife ran all the way back to friends at Bonney Well on Greenwood Station to tell them what had happened. Her family helped take Willaberta's body back to Greenwood Station for a ceremonial burial.

My family recall how word about Willaberta's death carried through the country like the wind. Many mourned the death of their local hero, while others, like the miners and pastoralists, thought that justice had been served.

My father is well known in the Territory as the one who created Willaberta Jack as a local Aboriginal hero. People still talk about the shooting to this day.

I was safe from the authorities until the fatal shooting of my father in 1928. From that day, my poor mother and relatives roamed the countryside trying to avoid the eyes of the authorities.

The Bungalow

The Bungalow was a government-funded institution established to accommodate and train half-caste children with the skills that would eventually enable them to take their places in the community once they were aged eighteen.

Half-caste girls especially were put into government institutions like the Alice Springs Bungalow as soon as possible after reaching an age when they could be separated from their Aboriginal mothers.

I was one of the children who were taken into the care, custody and control of the Director of Native Affairs under Section 6 of the *Aboriginals Ordinance 1918–47*.

Section 6(1) of the ordinance stated that 'the Chief Protector shall be entitled at anytime to undertake the care, custody, or control of any aboriginal or half-caste if, in his opinion it is necessary or desirable in the interests of the aboriginal or half-caste for him to do so, and for that purpose may enter any premises where the aboriginal or half-caste is or is supposed to be, and may take him into his custody.' This gave the Director of Native Affairs unlimited powers over part-Aborigines or half-castes like me, and made it legal for the authorities to take children from their parents or families at the request or direction of the Director.

I didn't know it then, but the Director of Native Welfare became my legal guardian the day I was taken from my mother and arrived at the Bungalow.

I can't remember any part of the journey to the Bungalow. Yet I do recall arriving there. I can still remember seeing the gumtree in the yard as the ute stopped in front of a house. The driver got out and came around the back. He lifted me out and left me standing there while he disappeared inside the house. After a while he came out, hopped into the ute and drove away. I couldn't understand why he was leaving me and not taking me back to where we'd come from. I remember running after the ute as it disappeared, but someone stopped me from following.

The Bungalow became my new home, and I would never see my mother again. To this day I don't understand why I can't remember being taken away from my family. A dear friend of mine, Mrs Pearl Powell, (who lived with her parents at Barrow Creek Station in the 1900s) knew my father through his visits to see her parents, and to collect mail and food. Pearl suggested that it might have been that my mother witnessing my father being shot that triggered the loss of memory, or her state of grief when she learnt of his death. It seemed so odd to both of us that I was able to remember arriving at the Bungalow.

I believe that I will find the answer to my loss of memory one day and hopefully my family research will help me piece together the missing years of my childhood.

Our sleeping quarters in the Bungalow was a dormitory. The beds were bunk style and we all had our own beds with the girls and boys in separate dormitories.

It didn't take me long to make friends with the other children there and soon my loneliness was replaced with laughter and happiness.

My friends Netta and Jessie Waters told me much later in life that when I arrived at the Bungalow I had very long hair, but that not long after my arrival my hair was cut off by one of the staff.

I remember the rabbits we kept as pets. We would dig holes for them in the banks of the creek beds, but somehow they always dug themselves out. It wasn't until much later that we could work this out. Then there was Easter. I remember a particular occasion when someone slid a piece of paper under the classroom door. The teacher asked one of the children to pick up the note and bring it to her. She read it aloud: 'Easter Bunny has hidden some eggs in the hill where the tank is, let's go and find them.' We climbed all over the hill looking for the eggs until we all found one each and sat down happily eating them.

I also loved galloping along on syrup tin lids with string, making out that I was riding a horse, making believe that the strings were the horse's reins. I neighed realistically, and shied at imagined objects, just as I'd seen horses do in the movies. I can still remember being taken to the movies in Alice Springs with other children from the Bungalow as a special treat. These were my fondest memories.

I can still see our favourite swimming hole adjacent to the home, at the bottom of a hill. One day some of us wanted to swim just like the bigger girls and we asked them if they would teach us.

They agreed, so half a dozen of us smaller children climbed the rock and waited. One of the older girls demonstrated how to dog paddle. We watched as she waded into the water and showed us the movements. Then she climbed up the rock to where we were sitting and pushed us in, one by one.

When we were all in the water trying to dog-paddle she called out, 'There's a deep hole under the rock and if you don't swim fast enough big hands will drag you under and keep you there.' I dog-paddled for my dear life. I was so scared of being dragged under by the big hands that I beat most of the other kids to the other side of the creek. When I reached the bank I lay on the sand getting my breath back and watching the other kids swimming for their lives.

We all learnt how to dog-paddle really fast that day. Although we were traumatised in the process, we were very pleased with ourselves. I also remember another day when we were swimming in the waterhole like little dogs. Someone cried out, 'Florrie's sinking, the big hands have got her!' Ruby Braun, who was swimming next to Florrie (Barrow), grabbed Florrie's arm and pulled her out to safety. Someone asked, 'How big were the hands Florrie?' Poor Florrie couldn't talk, and she looked pretty scared and shaken up to me. We all went home thankful that she was safe. I didn't go swimming there anymore. I kept out of the waterhole, but I sure did miss swimming.

I still think back to a time when I was playing with some of the other children in the yard outside. One of the children came over to a boy called Jack Clancy and told him that both his mother and mine were up the hill and wanted to see us. I remember walking up the hill with Jack. When we reached the area where our mothers were waiting Jack went and sat on his mother's lap and I saw her give him a packet of biscuits. I remember standing there just looking at them, wondering which was my mother. I couldn't remember her. I still ask myself today, 'How could I have forgotten my mother. Children never forget their mothers.'

I've been back to the Bungalow a couple of times since my childhood. The last time was with two of my daughters and a few of my grandchildren, to show them where I'd grown up. I found the hills where we'd searched for our Easter eggs. The hills, so large to me as a child, turned out to be no more than a mound. It was a shock to me.

I also remembered the red stones we found in the dirt at the back of the school, under the pepper-berry tree. When playing marbles we'd clear the dirt away and unearth red stones. They were very bright red in colour. We were excited and raced in to show our teacher. She'd say to us, 'If you find any more, bring them to me and I'll give you oranges and boiled lollies'. It would be funny, with kids running around screaming out in delight, 'I found one, I found one. Hey it's bright red just like the teacher's lipstick.' The teachers would give us a boiled lolly or half an orange for each 'red stone' that we found. It was only after we had grown up that some of us realised that the red stones must have been of really valuable to the staff, particularly as they kept rewarding us with boiled lollies for each one we found. Some said the stones were rubies, others said they were amethysts.

News of the War

The news of the World War Two came and we learned that the Japanese and Germans were our enemies. I remember that we had a large map of the world on the classroom wall and there were little flags portraying each country, especially the countries at war.

Each morning our teacher, Miss Penry, would move the flags on the map and let us know how close the war was to Australia, and what was happening in England. Like so many of the other children, I didn't quite understand the war, but it made us scared when we saw the flags getting close to Australia. Alice Springs had become a military town and throughout 1941 urgent efforts were made to place us children somewhere safe and out of the Army's way. Families in the Alice Springs area were told to collect their children from the Bungalow, while others like me, with our mothers hundreds of miles away in the bush, were moved to various islands in the north.

On 26 May 1941 the truck set off from Alice Springs with its first party of thirty-eight children. Some of the children suffered from trachoma on the trip to Darwin.

The Roman Catholic Church made plans to take their children to Bathurst Island, and the Anglicans took their children to Groote Eylandt. The Methodists, who had the largest group of all and were strongly opposed to the idea of mixing half-caste children with full-blood children, decided to establish a special settlement for our group on Croker Island.

I remember travelling by road in trucks all the way to Darwin; I can still see us quite clearly. We girls were wearing pretty new bonnets and the boys wearing whatever they were given. We were told that it would be very hot up in the Top End.

Reaching Birdum we all hopped onto the train and travelled to Darwin. Once settled in Darwin we were taken to the Botanical Gardens. It was here at the gardens that we first saw coconuts and tasted the milk. Some of the children scrambled up the palms like monkeys. The coconuts didn't stay up there for very long.

During our stopover in Darwin, we travelled in the Native Affairs boat *Aroetta* to a small Aboriginal community across the bay from Darwin. It was called Delissaville, and is now known as Belyuen. While there, we were told not to go near the Army because they were building a new road. It was on this trip that we tasted salt water for the very first time. I still remember how the salt burnt my mouth and how I spat it out as quickly as I could. I was convinced that hundreds of bags of salt had been poured into the sea. I couldn't believe water could be so salty.

I remember the day we left Darwin for Goulburn Island. As the boat was pulling away from the wharf my friend Netta Waters looked at me and said as she pointed in the direction of the wharf, 'Look Clara. Wave, wave.'

Netta was pointing to someone she knew who was on the wharf. The person was waving to us. I wouldn't look back to the wharf. Netta prompted me again. 'Hey come on Clara, look, she's still there, wave'.

I answered her, 'No, I don't want to turn around and look at her because I might turn into a pillar of salt like Lot's wife.' I remembered the story in the Bible how Lot's wife turned into a pillar of salt because she was warned not to look back and she did. I remembered from our religious instruction classes at school, how Lot, his wife and two daughters fled from Sodom, the doomed city. Lot said to them, 'Don't look back', but his wife looked back longingly and was turned into a pillar of salt. I believed that this would happen to me if I looked back.

Many of the children, including me, were seasick for most of the first leg of our trip. When we reached Melville Island we were told that we couldn't get off the boat because it was a Catholic Mission. So the boat had to anchor in Fish Creek and we slept on board.

The next morning the boat pulled anchor and we were on our way again to our next destination. Many of us were seasick again. The rocking of the boat, the smell of the sea and the diesel were no help to us.

The boat anchored in Bowen Strait between Croker Island and the mainland. Mr Reuben Cooper had his sawmill on the mainland and this was where we all were able to get rid of our seasickness for a while.

When it was time to leave the mainland, we were driven down to the beach and then men had to carry us to the dinghies to save us from getting wet.

This day was the very first time after being in the Bungalow, that we'd laid eyes on a full-blood Aboriginal. Stephen Colbert (who has now passed away) said as he stared at two Aboriginal men, 'They're real black!' He just couldn't believe his eyes. 'They're black as the ace of spades.' One of the staff overheard him and said, 'Stephen that's not a very nice thing to say.' Stephen just kept repeating, 'They're real black!'

Stephen was so preoccupied with the darkness of the men he didn't notice they were wearing only nagas at the time. Others of us were shocked at their clothing, because we hadn't seen anyone dressed like that before.

Claire Henty-Gebert — me at the age of 17 years on Croker Island, 1947.

Some of us girls on Croker Island. (Back) Nancy Cameron and Lily Kunoth, (front) Queenie Farrar (deceased) and Claire Henty, c. 1940s.

Sergeant Harry Henty, 12th Battalion, was recommended for the Military Medal for action in 1917 at Bullecourt.

Ruins of Hatches Creek School, Northern Territory, 1968.

George Birchmore, Ted Martin and Harry Henty, my father, standing in front of the Barrow Creek Telegraph Station, c. 1920. Courtesy Mortlock South Australiana Collection, State Library of South Australia.

Dormitory girls on Croker Island, 1948. (Left to right) Audrey Waters, Linda Vale, Jessie Waters, Claire Henty, Claudette Tanami, Nancy Cameron, and (front) Ruby Braun.

Standing outside a teacher's residence. (Left to right) Queenie Farrar (deceased), Mrs Greentree, Dolly Scrymgour (deceased) and Linda Vale, c. 1940s.

Another great day of fishing at Japanese Creek, Croker Island with (left to right) Bob and Amy Randall, and Stephen Colbert (deceased) and Bill Patterson (front) 1954.

On the beach, Croker Island. 1955. (Left to right) Eileen Smith holding my daughter, Cyndia; Peggy Taylor holding my youngest daughter, Deanna, with Margret Gray holding the dog, and Barbara Wauchope in the arms of April Clayton.

Croker Island missionaries and children after the war, 1950.

Children and missionaries ready for an outing. Mr Rupert Kentish (deceased) standing at door of truck, Croker Island, 1948.

Larrpan I *anchored at old Stokes Hill Wharf, Darwin, 1949.*

(Clockwise from front) Leslie Jones, Stephen Colbert, Teddy Hayes, Max Cummings and James Grant on the old blitz truck after a day of shooting, Croker Island, 1951.

Photo taken before the war of children and missionaries on the boat Kalami *anchored at Delisaville (now known as Belyuen) which is situated across the Darwin harbour, 1941.*

Hill view of Croker Island Mission, 1948.

(Left to right) Queenie Farrar (deceased), Pauline Shepherd, Lorna Tennant Fejo, Betty Harvey and Ruby Braun Roe collecting water lilies on Croker Island after the war, 1949.

Cyril Frith and Bob Shepherd sawing timber on Croker Island.

The missionary children tended the peanut and paw paw garden, Croker Island Mission, 1948.

Boys looking after goats, Croker Island, 1948.

My younger brother and Harry Henty's son, Dick Tennant (deceased) looking through the ruins of the American Liberator, Croker Island.

Me, Candice Coles and Netta Cahill at the goat stockyard at the bungalow, Alice Springs.

The cattle on Croker Island provided food to the Mission, 1950.

The boat's engine started and we all turned our attention to the beach and waved to the men who had helped us into the dinghies. The boat then headed for Goulburn Island. It was at the end of 1941 and we were to stay at Goulburn Island on a temporary basis, until the houses on Croker Island were ready for us. There were forty children from Pine Creek, twenty-eight from Alice Springs and another twenty or more were kept in Darwin for medical treatment. These children joined our group at Goulburn Island later.

Mr Keith Wale was appointed as the Superintendent to oversee the missionaries and their work at Goulburn Island and also to supervise our relocation to Croker Island. He and his wife transferred from Milingimbi to Goulburn Island. Mr and Mrs Wale, Miss Olive Peak and Miss Jess March were employed by the Methodist Overseas Mission church to care for us. The sudden influx of people at Goulburn Island meant that the staff had to find food for nearly a hundred extra mouths. Cattle were driven from Oenpelli to the beach where they were shot, skinned, and loaded on the motorboat. The carcasses were then brought across to Goulburn Island to feed us. Some of us were told wild pigs were brought from Croker Island for extra food and that they were kept in pens, until needed. I never saw the pigs, but certainly heard them on occasions.

We attended school at Goulburn Island and in addition to the three Rs were also taught to weave pandanus mats and baskets by some of the local Aboriginal women. They also took groups of us out into the bush in small expeditions to collect the raw materials for the weaving. The women taught us to pull out the pandanus shoots, strip each 'slot' and hang the strips up to dry, ready for use in our next weaving lessons.

In early November 1941, Miss Somerville, the daughter of a Methodist parson, arrived on staff. Miss Somerville said that she had read an appeal in the *Missionary Review* for six sewing machines for the new work at Croker Island. She had a spare sewing machine so she took it with her to the Methodist Headquarters in Sydney to make her offer. She said that while she was being interviewed one thing led to another and, in the end, she decided to take the sewing machine to Goulburn Island personally. She didn't know it then, but she would stay with us as a missionary for more than twenty years.

On 25 November 1941 the *Larrpan* made another journey. This time it carried an advance party of forty-four children with Mr and Mrs Wale, Miss Olive Peak and Sister Somerville from Goulburn Island to Croker Island. The *Larrpan* then returned to Goulburn to collect Miss Jess March and Fuata Taito and his family.

Mr Adams had the difficult task of preparing to accommodate one hundred children and staff. Under war conditions, supplies and transport were in short supply, but he stuck to his job. By the time of our arrival, the building crew had completed nearly four cottages, though none had floors.

No sooner had we moved in than the rain came: thirteen inches in one night. The floors turned into mud. The makeshift beds floated and most of the children turned their beds into boats and made mud pies.

We'd hardly settled on the island when news of the Japanese attack on Pearl Harbor stunned the world. This was 8 December (Australian time) 1941.

On 16 December 1941, the Government ordered all women and children to leave Darwin. However, it wasn't until 13 February 1942 that a radio message was sent along the coast by the Methodist Overseas Mission advising that all missionaries' wives and children were to be evacuated. The radio message also said that any other white women wanting to leave with them could do so. The evacuation for half-caste children was to come at a later date. This outraged Miss March, Sister Peak and Miss Somerville and they refused to leave us behind. Mr Wale also stayed with us. There were ninety-six children on the island.

Darwin was bombed by the Japanese at 10 o'clock on 19 February 1942. With Darwin being bombed there was no hope of any boat coming for us all, because the ships that had survived the harbour raid were desperately needed for the troops. The Department of Native Affairs could tell the missionaries nothing. So the staff unpacked and we resumed school again. However, the staff remained uneasy because Croker Island was on the air route between the enemy base and Darwin, and war planes flew over daily.

One evening when the radio worked, the missionaries were shocked to hear that cows were being evacuated from some parts of the north. They couldn't believe what they were hearing.

They said they would have liked to ask if we ninety-six children in the path of enemy bombers weren't more important than cows.

The following day, staff called us together to advise that they had received a message on the pedal radio that everyone on the island was to collect stones and make a large cross in a cleared area. The girls carried stones in the skirts of their dresses and made lots of trips to a cleared site. The boys collected as much as they could carry in their hands and arms.

We laid the stones down on what emerged as the shape of a cross. Everyone helped clear the area around the cross so that it could be seen from the sky. Once the stones were laid and the cross completed, it was painted white. We all worked very late into the night. The cross was our sign to the aircrews flying over the island that it was a mission station.

The next day after breakfast we went to look at our work. The cross was painted white and looked very good. I thought surely the aircrews in the planes couldn't miss seeing it. That night in bed we chatted away, each of us admitting how scared we were, especially when we were told that Croker Island was on the air route between the enemy base and Darwin. Whenever we played we kept a constant lookout for planes. The missionaries warned us that if we saw a plane with the rising sun on the side of the plane and its wings it would be the enemy, the Japanese.

Each time we saw a plane someone would shout 'Japs' and we'd run for cover. If we were close to the jungle or thick bushes we'd hide in the foliage. If not, we lay flat on our tummies and kept still.

Sister Olive Peak and Sister Somerville found a safe place for us to hide from the Japanese. The hideout was up the hill, behind the mission. It was well located and a large hole was dug into which we shoved crates of tinned food. We learned later that some of the boys who knew where the food was hidden were going up to the hill to eat the food. They'd then neatly pack the crates as though nothing had been touched. The missionaries soon learnt what was happening and the crates were bought down to the store again. So much for the good plan. Of course, the boys were reprimanded for their mischief.

On one particular day I went to Japanese Creek with some other children to swim. We took something to eat and a bag of Rickett's blue, which is an antidote for jelly fish stings. Rickett's Blue burnt the jellyfish tentacles and numbed the pain. The only reminder of the sting is a dark outline on the skin where the tentacles had clung tightly to the body. Japanese Creek was half a mile away from the mission. The creek was used by the Japanese and Malay fishermen to shelter in the heavy storms during their fishing expeditions for trepang or bêche-de-mer which was a delicacy to Japanese and Malaysian people. Trepang is a long black thing that looks like a cucumber; when touched, it wriggles like snake. The Japanese and Malays lefttheir trademark bamboo wells at the bottom of cliffs to catch the springwater trickling down the cliff-face. The water was icy cold and refreshing to drink on hot days. We used the clay at the bottom of the cliffs for moulding into shapes of animals.

Anyway, on one particular day some of us were swimming while others sat under a small bushy tree close to the creek. During our laughing and splashing water at each other we heard the droning sound of a plane. 'Plane!' someone shouted. 'It's coming here and it's coming straight at us!' Those of us in the water took deep breaths and ducked under the water. I don't know why, but before I ducked my head under the water, I looked straight up at the plane and noticed the pilot wearing goggles. His hand was on something as the plane dived low. I called out to the others 'Oh no! He's going to shoot us. We're going to die.' It seemed like ages before one of the children sitting under the tree came and told us the plane had gone, that the plane was actually one of ours. We couldn't get out of the water fast enough. We raced back to the mission, sticking as close as we could to the trees, and reminding each other that we were to lie flat on our tummies, if the plane returned. Arriving at the mission, we told one of the staff what had happened. We described how we'd held our breath under the water until the plane flew away, while the others huddled under the little bushy tree on the beach. After that incident we all had to stay around the mission. The planes would frequently fly over Croker, swoop down and head off towards Darwin.

On Good Friday, 3 April 1942, Mr Adam's wife gave birth to their baby daughter, Rosemary, at Croker Island. Four days later, we were all packed and we left Croker for the mainland. This was the first part of our long trek to New South Wales.

I still remember our Good Friday service at nine o'clock in the morning. We all stood around the large white cross we'd laid and painted. The sky was so beautiful that morning, it changed from grey to red as the sun rose like a fiery ball over the quiet waters of Croker Bay. There was a feeling of sadness amongst us all, especially the children, after being told that we would be leaving our home, Croker. The place that we had all come to love.

The *Larrpan 1* arrived at two o'clock, bringing Reverend Len Kentish from Goulburn Island and Mr Jim Harris from Oenpelli. They had come to help us on our journey. I watched the sky for Japanese planes, scared that they'd soon come and blast us out of existence. I prayed and prayed that day, that they wouldn't come.

Who could have foretold that within four months of our arrival on Croker that we'd be on the move again — and this time interstate?

The long trek south

On approximately 8 April 1942, we were carried in dinghies and canoes to the *Larrpan 1*, anchored out in Croker Bay. As we sailed away from Croker we were all waving and saying, 'Goodbye Croker. We'll come home when the War is over.' We didn't have any flowers to send back on the waves to the shore. The Fijian families had taught us that this was their way of saying goodbye to the place you were leaving, and we wanted to do the same. It made us very sad to leave the place we all loved so much. I can still see myself crying with the other girls, wiping our tears away with the hems of our skirts. We were leaving our home and it was a very sad occasion for all of us. As the *Larrpan 1* cut its way through the blue waters, we saw a lot of colourful water snakes, turtles and flying fish. At the same time most of us still kept a watchful eye out for enemy planes.

By darkness we reached Barclay Point on the mainland. Once we'd all disembarked we were given blankets and sleeping bags made from sheets. We were all so tired that we slept on the beach. It must have been a sight: ninety-six children strewn over the beach in sleeping bags and blankets. The next morning a utility and truck came to pick us up and drive us to Oenpelli. The smaller children went in the vehicles, but the older ones, including me, walked behind the trucks. We ended up with a lot of spear grass in our clothes and hair. I can still see myself, just like it was yesterday, skipping along and singing 'Telephone to Glory', to keep myself from getting tired along the way.

This kept me awake and whenever I felt tired I'd carry on singing again. Eventually though that didn't last, and those of us who were tired were carried by the others until we were able to walk again, or the trucks stopped for a rest. We picked wild plums, gooseberries and billy-goat plums (the green flat ones) and sucked the juice out of the water grass which was very sweet. The water grass produced assorted flavours like cordials. It was a godsend because it quenched our thirst along the way.

Oenpelli

Arriving at Oenpelli, I couldn't help but notice how pictur-esque it was. It had hills in the background and reflected in the lagoon and with cattle grazing. Little birds with red legs walked daintily on the water lilies which bloomed on top of the water. It was breathtaking.

Although only a child at the time, I could see the beauty of the area. Once we'd settled in at the mission many of the other children jumped into a nearby lagoon, pulling out the stems of the lilies, and eating them. I didn't join them because I was scared of snakes and leeches.

The next morning after breakfast we were all given chores to do. After my chores I raced some of the other children down to the billabong. It was really pretty, just like the pic-tures I'd seen books.

Some of the other children raced into the water with their clothes on, but not me. One of the children called out to the others warning them to keep a lookout for snakes. Some of the children raced out, soaking wet, picking up sticks and stones and using them as missiles to chase that kid.

We had our sad times at Oenpelli too. One day one of our young boys, only four-and-a-half years old, died after an acci-dent. Sister Peak tried hard to save his life. She even radioed Darwin seeking assistance, but to no avail. His name was Charlie Hayes and he was laid to rest in the Oenpelli cemetery, under the shade of Mt Argalook. There's still a little white cross with the inscription: 'Charles Hayes at 4½ years — Croker Islander.' That morning has remained with me to this day. I've never been back to the gravesite, but hope that one day I'll make the journey. Some of the other Croker Islanders later returned as adults.

On 27 April 1942, at 7.30 we left Oenpelli for Pine Creek. We travelled for several miles to the East Alligator River. The river was known to be tidal, so we had to be taken across in canoes. During the canoe trips our eyes scanned the river looking for crocodiles. We all feared the canoes tipping over and spilling us into the river.

There were full-blood Aboriginals walking waist deep in the water on either side of the canoes and they helped get us across the river by guiding the canoes. The truck was driven down the creek to a steep bank and manoeuvred into position on a makeshift raft made out of six empty four-gallon petrol drums lashed together with board and ropes. The vehicle was securely perched on the raft and the men pushed and pulled it to the other side.

After the epic crossing we walked a further two and a half miles across 'devil-devil' country as we called it, until we arrived at Sandy Creek. How could I forget Sandy Creek. The mosquitoes! They attacked us from all sides. Even the smoke from the fires couldn't keep them away. We covered our heads and bodies with blankets to keep the mozzies out, but it wasn't any good. How glad we were to see morning. With breakfast over we were ready again. We children, all aged about eight to ten years of age, spread out across the countryside. The distance was close to thirteen miles by road. It makes me wonder now how we walked that far, as we were so young. During our trek Miss March and Sister Somerville tried to sing with us, but the singing didn't last as we tired. When thirsty we'd brush aside the green scum from the stagnant ponds along the way and drink the water. We also looked for bush tucker. We found plums, water grass and gooseberries.

We ate the fruit as quickly as we found it, never forgetting to offer some to Miss March and Miss Somerville.

Mr Wale found two small children up a tree looking for the first group they belonged with. Thank goodness Mr Wale found them. On another occasion during a head count he stopped and called out, 'Where's Betty Fisher?' Betty was missing. Mr Wale galloped back to our last resting place, calling out and searching for her. He found her asleep in the long grass. We were happy to have her back with us. She told us she'd been tired, had curled up and gone to sleep. She made us all laugh when she told us how her little legs couldn't wrap around the belly of Mr Wale's horse; they were just hanging, flapping on the side of the horse.

Approximately eighteen miles from Nourlangie, Reverend Toft, the Methodist Minister from Darwin, and another missionary, Mr Harris, arrived in their lorries, bringing mail for the staff and to help us make the final journey to Nourlangie, where we were to meet the government trucks.

That night we reached our destination. The trucks sent out by the Department of Native Affairs in Darwin arrived to meet us. Five lorries were to take us to our next stop.

With this part of the journey over, Reverend Len Kentish was getting ready to return to Oenpelli to look after things at the mission until he could be joined by Mr Harris. We all liked Mr Kentish; he was a very special man to us. I remember waving to him with the other children, bidding him farewell as he rode into the distance. We didn't know it then, but that would be the last time we'd see him alive. Some time after we settled in Sydney we were told that a few weeks after we'd seen him, he'd been captured by the Japanese and beheaded. The missionaries told one of the other children that he'd been taken to a Japanese-held island called Dobo in the Aru Islands, now part of Indonesia. That was a very sad day for us and we hated the Japanese very much that day. I still carry that sadness to this day.

Our journey took us past Jim Jim, Mary River and then on to Pine Creek. At Pine Creek we received word that the American military had taken over the place, so we had to camp outside the town boundaries under some trees. The area was known as Butchers Paddock and it was here that we waited for the weekly train.

The American soldiers were very good to us. Our camp was made 'out of bounds', and they gave us a guard to watch over us every night. Bombing raids were conducted over Darwin every day now, and enemy planes were coming down over Pine Creek and as far south as Katherine.

During our short stopover, at the request of the American soldiers we presented a concert which everyone enjoyed and the American soldiers appreciated. We sang and Sister Somerville recited. One of the Americans said to Mr Toft that he was very surprised at our English, especially Sister Somerville's. He said that she spoke better English than he did. Sister Somerville's skin had become very dark from exposure to the hot sun and he'd thought she was one of us. We all giggled at this.

The next morning we had to get up early to leave at 7 o'clock for Pine Creek, then Birdum. When we awoke the staff were already cooking breakfast and preparing for the forthcoming journey.

The military helped the missionaries by looking after us and cooking. They cooked dampers, fried scones, rice and beef in a kerosene tin. One of the children was surprised, 'Hey, look, they can cook dampers!' After breakfast we bathed and were given clean clothes for the journey. The staff were told by the locals in Pine Creek that we were the last and largest party of women and children to leave the north.

From trucks to trains

At Birdum we were transferred to cattle trucks and lorries as there were no railway tracks to Alice Springs. We began our southward journey along the Stuart Highway, under military escort. When we needed to go to the toilet we knocked on the roof of the trucks. The drivers would pull over and stop the vehicles. We'd all jump out and the driver would take a head count. Then we'd all rush to the bush, some to relieve themselves and others to pick bush fruit and berries. During these stops, the drivers would stretch their legs, have a yarn and a smoke. On our return, heads would be counted again. Knocks on the roof of the trucks happened quite often along the highway, as did the baggage rolling about in the back of the trucks.

If I ever had the opportunity to meet those drivers and the American soldiers who helped us in Pine Creek, I'd thank them for looking after us.

On our arrival in Alice Springs the staff were told there was no room in the Bungalow for us because it was occupied by other evacuee groups so we erected tents in the dry creek bed nearby and slept there. During the day we had enough time to get together with some of the friends we had grown up with in the Bungalow, before the War.

Meat and bread were delivered each day to our camp. The staff and the older children cooked on the open fire and we ate picnic style. One Friday night at six o'clock we were piled into three large military trucks. We waved to our friends at the

Bungalow and left for the railway station where carriages had been reserved for us on the train bound for Adelaide. I still remember how we were all dressed in summer clothes and as the train edged closer south how we began to feel cold.

Oodnadatta was the first place we came to, followed by Maree and then Quorn, where our party was met at the railway station by local parishioners and taken to the local town hall to eat. People even gave us pennies as gifts. I put all mine in my pillow case for safe-keeping. I never got the chance to spend my pennies, because when the train reached Sydney I was one of the children to stay in Sydney. My pillowcase and pennies continued on with the other children to Otford. I always wondered who ended up enjoying my pennies.

From Quorn we travelled onto Yerowie where we changed trains. The Red Cross kindly served us breakfast and Olive Peak's parents, who lived at Nhil, were there to meet the train at 3 o'clock in the morning. It was pitch black and so cold.

Our next stop was Melbourne and most of us felt frozen from the cold. We were given warm clothes and blankets, but this still didn't keep out the chill or stop our teeth from chattering. When the train reached Albury, a small country town on the New South Wales border, we were met by Reverend H. H. Allen and a few other church people. They provided a mobile canteen and gave us hot tea and sandwiches. The train then left for the final stage of our journey to Sydney. In our carriage we had plenty of space to sleep and we slept on the floor, seats and anywhere else we could put our little bodies. However, with all the cold weather some of us were sick with influenza, diarrhoea and sore eyes. Canberra was next and then there was another change of trains to Sydney. At last we arrived at Sydney's Central Station around midday. Sister Somerville was very happy to see her family again. We had lunch in the Social Hall of the Headquarters of the Methodist Church in Castlereagh Street.

Wishing to help, Sister Somerville's father kept us entertained by taking us for rides in the lift. The ride was new and exciting for us. Poor man, I hope we behaved ourselves. Some of us had come to the end of our journey and the staff set about splitting us into two groups. I went with twenty other children to George Brown College in Haberfield. The group of children included Ruby Braun, Betty Fisher, Alice Carrol (now Bristow), Jessie Waters (now Lyons), Betty Harvey (the late Betty Wauchope), Lorna Tennant (now Fejo), Polly Dean, Mattie Frith and Hazel Burton. I hope I haven't left many names out. We all went to school at Haberfield Public Primary. The other seventy-six children and staff caught the train down to Otford, a township nestling among the hills on the south coast of New South Wales. The Methodist Crusader Movement owned a property in Otford which was used for study and recreational camps and it became home to the other children from Croker Island, during the War.

During our stay at George Brown College we found out that there was a room in the college that was kept for the Queen of Tonga, Queen Salote, whenever she visited Sydney. I'll never forget when two of the girls told me and a couple of other girls that they had seen Queen Salote's bed. They couldn't get over the size of her bed and chair, describing it as the biggest bed and chair that they'd ever seen. They described the bed by stretching their arms out as far as they could extend them. One of our girls said to the others, 'You're gammon, you're making it up'. The storyteller responded by saying (demonstrating her Hail Marys) 'cross my heart'. The other girl said, 'Yes, it's true'. Apparently the girls were able to have a sneak look while the housemaid was cleaning the room. Their eyes were really big as they told us what they'd seen. We were in awe. I badly wanted to see Queen Salote's bed and chair to see if the other girls were telling the truth, but I never got the chance.

I remember sneaking along the hallway with another girl, fingers crossed, hoping that the door would be open, just a little, so that we could have a peep. Fancy wishing so hard for something. We never got our wish. When we arrived in Otford the story was retold there, over and over again.

Some time later, those of us at George Brown's College travelled to Otford to join the other children. The staff looking after us had been told that the church needed the space to train more missionaries. In Otford, some of us attended the local public school while others attended Scarborough. In our more senior years many of the older girls attended Wollongong Home Science High School. We also went to Burwood High School once a week for cooking classes. I was in Year 2AH and I enjoyed my school days in Otford. I found it easy to make friends with the local children who were friendly and, of course, curious about us.

I still have a good laugh when I think of a funny incident. I'd just finished classes on one particular day and was walking to the station with my best friend Valda, a young white girl, along with some of the Croker Island girls, when a young white girl came up to us. (I always thought the girl was Nida Wilson but when I asked her she said it wasn't.) She asked, 'Did your father kill Captain Cook and eat him?' One girl in our group responded quickly and said, 'No, but I'm going to eat you!' The Croker girl dropped her school bag and chased after the young girl. We were all speechless, but you should have seen the look on that young girl's face. She ran as fast as she could, with our girl hot in pursuit. I bet that young white girl could have won an Olympic gold medal that day. I looked for her at school the next day, but I couldn't see her.

On 4 July 1944, Mr Adams and Mr Rupert Kentish, a missionary from Yirrkala, returned to Croker Island with three Fijian missionaries, Fuata, Kolinio and Aminias. They were on leave at the time and were to begin building new houses in time for our return to the island. The men were accompanied by eight of our boys including Bill Ryan, James Ryan, James Wauchope, Jack Scrymgour. The boys were all aged between 11 and 13 years of age.

It wasn't until two years later that we were told that the War was over. We were happy because this meant that we could return home to Croker Island.

On 4 April 1946 we left Otford to begin our journey back to the island. The memories of the friends we made in Otford still remain with many of us. From Otford we travelled to Sydney by train. There we boarded a special bus which took us to Circular Quay. There we boarded the *M.V. Reynella*, a 9000 ton vessel, formerly known as the Italian vessel *Remo*. Prior to its capture by the British, it was used as a passenger ship with accommodation for 300 travellers. Under the British it was used for transporting cargo but during the War it was converted to a troopship carrier.

The night before we were to sail there was a dispute on the dock and our departure was delayed. I can still remember some of us peeping out of the portholes and hearing one of the children yell out loud, 'Hey, there's fish down there'. I peeped out of the porthole to see one of the boys point down to the waterline. I looked down and saw lots of tiny fish swimming near the ship. Then someone said, 'Hey let's ask the men on the wharf for some bait and we'll ask the sailors for some lines.' Another answered, 'Alright, but you ask.' One of the boys called out to the man on the dock, 'Hey man, can we have some bait, please?' The man replied, 'Catch it.' Everyone screamed with fright as the man threw what we thought at the time was bait. But then we saw that it wasn't slippery slimy 'bait' but 'eating dates'. We all screamed with joy. We soon forgot about fishing and were scrambling on the cabin floors snatching what dates we could grab for ourselves. The men on the dock kept throwing dates at us as we hung out of the portholes. It was raining dates and we caught as many as we could in our small hands.

Early the next morning the staff woke to find us still in our nighties running to and from the portholes and back to our beds with handfuls of dried dates. On one occasion one of the men managed somehow to drop a box of dried fruit, smashing the casing. We believed this extra box was intended for us and sure enough it was. Dates and a mixture of dried fruit were everywhere, with the men handing over more to us as we hung out of our portholes. We hid the dried fruit in every corner of the cabin as well as in our pockets, under pillows, and in our suitcases. Tummy-aches followed, but the dates and other dried fruit kept popping up throughout the journey.

The ship's crew, from the Captain to deckhands, were very good to us. During the voyage from Sydney to Brisbane, we entertained the other passengers by giving a concert. I left the stage as soon as we had finished singing and returned to my cabin to eat more of the dried fruit. Some of the other children stayed behind with staff to talk to the passengers.

Some time later one of the other children came to the cabin to see me. 'Clara, Clara', she said. 'There's a passenger asking whether there is a girl called Clara Henty in our group.' The man had told some of the children that he had known my father and wanted to meet me. I was too scared to go and see him. He mentioned to the other children that his name was Burnett and that his family owned Burnett's Scrap Metal in Darwin. Silly me, I never followed that up. To this day I regret not talking to that gentleman.

On our journey home, the *Reynella* called into Brisbane. The Brisbane River was murky and its colour reminded me of brown coffee. We were on deck as someone pointed out the Glass House Mountains. It was beautiful and I thought of a pyramid cut from glass.

The *Reynella* anchored and we disembarked. Later that day we were taken by bus on a tour around Brisbane and out into the country. One place I remember was the pineapple factory. It had a large pineapple sitting up high and we could smell the pineapple juice as we neared the factory. We were given a grand tour of the factory and a glass of juice to drink.

I don't remember how long we stayed in Brisbane, but I guess it was only a couple of days; just long enough for the ship to fuel and load for the journey.

On Easter Monday, 22 April 1946, we said goodbye to the crew on the *Reynella* and boarded the boom defence vessel, the *Kangaroo*, to complete the journey to Croker Island. It was a rough trip and many of us were sick, but we all survived. Many days later as we neared our beloved Croker there was a cry of '*Larrpan*' from one of the children. Those of us still sick in bed soon rose to the occasion. Our dear old lugger the *Larrpan 1* had come out to the *Kangaroo*, to welcome us. We were all transferred from the *Kangaroo*, onto the *Larrpan 1* and ferried closer to shore. The voyage in the *Larrpan 1* was exciting and we were then ferried to the shore in dinghies.

Rupert Kentish and Phil Adams were there to meet us. Once we arrived at the mission we raced around examining the new homes. There were six cottages ready for us to move into.

Mr Kentish and the boys had developed a farm on land at the back of the cottages where they had planted tropical and citrus fruits and established a vegetable garden, as well as a goat yard and a pig sty. There were also hens, roosters and chickens.

Miss Daisy Craigen, a high school teacher from Wollongong, was employed to return to Croker with us. The education policy was to work towards the Intermediate standard for everyone at school. Many of us were in our second year at Wollongong Domestic Science High, when World War Two came to an end.

The school on Croker was an army masonite hut. I often have a chuckle talking about happenings on Croker with other former residents and can still remember two funny incidents. One of the children at the time, the late Harry North, whom we fondly nicknamed 'Northy Fella' would always interrupt our lessons. Whenever he heard the soft drone of an aeroplane approaching, he'd point his finger upwards and say, 'There!, There!, There!' and followed by a loud 'There!' He'd rise from his seat and race out of the classroom, looking up into the sky pointing upward and shouting excitedly, 'There! There!' He'd seem to forget about school and start running down to the airstrip, less than half a mile away. Other children would follow him, just as if he was the Pied Piper of Hamelin. Poor Miss Craigen would be left in the classroom with only a few students. School, of course, was finished for the day.

Next morning with Northy Fella in company we'd all turn up for school and say, 'Good morning, Miss Craigen' and she'd reply, 'Good morning, I hope everyone is ready for lessons today.' We'd all say politely, 'Yes Miss Craigen'. Northy Fella would act as though nothing had happened the day before.

The late John Hunter was the other colourful person in the class. We'd all hand in our compositions except John. Miss Craigen would give him an additional five minutes in which to hand in his work.

The next day during lessons, Miss Craigen would read out the compositions. As she came to the end of reading John's composition she'd find the words 'to be continued'. Every time, John couldn't think of how to finish off his composition, he would write the words 'to be continued'. Miss Craigen would say, 'John, you ended the last composition just like this!' He'd reply, 'I'll finish it next time Miss Craigen.' We would all start grinning, and then the giggles would begin. The following week John would finish his composition, but the week after, the next composition would end, 'to be continued'. John was really a very smart young man. He later became a light heavyweight boxer in the Northern Territory. He was believed to be heading for great heights in the boxing circles, but was tragically killed on a goose-shooting trip. Bob and Amy Randall and John's wife Pauline were with him that fatal day.

I still remember how Aboriginal people would fly and truck their way in to Darwin from the islands and communities, just to see John fight. John came to me to sew the name 'Hurricane Hunter' on the back of his gown. I felt very privileged that John had asked me. He was a dear friend of our family and we still have the memories of John in our hearts.

The school year came to an end and most of us passed our exams. The next task was to find work on the mission.

I joined some of the girls sewing and making sun frocks for the younger children. During my days at Wollongong High School I'd learnt to sew. I loved it and I did it well. We were paid 50 shillings a garment. I also attended Sister Somerville's art and craft classes. She taught us to make brooches from fish scales and shells. We made thousands and they were sold all over Australia and that's how we earned our pocket money. At the same time our achievements gave good publicity to Croker Island. We were all delighted to hear that Mrs Hasluck, later Lady Hasluck, wife of the then-Governor-General, the Honourable Paul Hasluck, was seen wearing a Croker Island brooch. We all wondered whose brooch she had worn.

The boys, on the other hand, did stock work. They also worked in the timber mill as well as with the mission's vehicles, and with the gardening.

The Aboriginal workers on the island, Timothy and Mick Yarmirr, told the boys how to recognise whether fruit was poisonous or non-poisonous, so that they could pass on their knowledge. We'd learnt about bush tucker when we were quite young and, as a rule, we passed on what we had learnt to the other children. The island had an abundance of wild fruit and vegetables. We were taught by the older boys that if we came across trees laden with fruit and there were masses of bruised and over ripe fruit on the ground, then it was not safe to eat.

We would always remind each other that if the birds wouldn't eat the fruit, then we shouldn't, because it was poisonous. I've passed down that knowledge to my own children and their children.

At times we walked to Second Bay where the mother turtles used to lay their eggs and then head back to the sea. We'd ride on the turtles' backs and scratch our names on their shells as they breast-stroked their way down the beach to the sea. We'd enter the sea with them, and fall off as they began to swim into deeper waters. We finish by frolicking with each other in the water closest to the shore.

We had lots of happy times on the island. But we also got into mischief like other children and were punished. Some of us were more mischievous than others. But not all of the missionaries on the island were bad. I know we had a better life on Croker than most other children in institutions in the Northern Territory.

My adolescent years were also memorable ones. I still remember overhearing a boy telling one of the girls a story about a 'kadaitja man'. It was on a day that a group of us were going swimming at Japanese Creek. He said to one of the girls in our group, 'Hey you girls, be careful if you come across a native dodging from tree to tree with all his body painted up and with feathers on his hair and his feet so that he can cover his tracks. But, don't you lot be scared because he's hunting someone else, not you lot.'

I heard this, but didn't take much notice and kept walking with the other girls. On the way to Japanese Creek one of the girls said, 'Hey you lot, we better be careful and look out for that kadaitja man with the paint on his body and feathers on his feet.'

We all responded, 'Yeah okay.'

Nearing the airstrip on our way home, one the girls whispered, 'Hey, I just saw a kadaitja man dodging from tree to tree. We all looked at each other, frozen, our eyes big, like saucers. The same girl said, 'He's over there.' She indicated with her eyes. She said, 'I saw him dodge from one tree to another tree. Now he's going to the third tree.' We were all walking really fast by now, and were too frightened to look over towards the trees. One of the other girls said, 'Yeah, but he's not hunting us, he's after someone else!' This detail didn't matter to us. After crossing the airstrip we raced home. I remember hearing someone call out behind me, 'Hey, don't leave me behind' but I just kept running until I reached the mission. It was a really frightening time. After that we stopped going to Japanese Creek for quite awhile. I reckon we could have broken a world record that day.

A few days later the news spread about the mission that the kadjaitja man and other Aboriginal men who were hunting a man were going to punish him, Aboriginal way. I believe it was because he had taken the wife of a man from another island. The boys told us where and when the punishment would take place. One of the girls said, 'Hey Claire do you want to come with us? They're going to punish the man that they've been hunting.' Someone else said, 'We can't go down on the beach, so we'll sit up on the cliff and watch, then take off when it's finished.' I was eager and agreed to go with the other girls. We all felt sorry for the Aboriginal man who was going to be punished because we liked him.

We watched from the cliffs in fear as he dodged every spear that was thrown at him. After the 'pay back' business the other Aboriginal men left the area. We went home happy because the man was now free of any more punishment and was able to live with his wife in peace.

There was also the time when one of the boys, Ronald Roberts, made a guitar out of wood. Some of the children teased him about the shape of guitar because it looked like a watermelon. Many of the children called it the 'watermelon guitar'. Ron didn't seem to mind all the teasing from the others because he got many enjoyable hours using it.

He wanted to learn how to play the guitar properly so he asked Violet Liddy to help him write a letter to Tex Morton's manager because he wanted a book of Tex Morton's music. Tex Morton was a well-known country and western singer in those days. Some months later, to his surprise Ron received the book of sheet music. Ron was determined to play the guitar and he did.

I guess it was Ron's determination, intelligence, humour and likable nature that attracted me to him. He was very popular with those who knew him on the island.

I was later to marry him. On 27 March 1951 Ronald Roberts and I were married on Croker Island. We had three daughters. Our two eldest daughters were born while we were still living on the island. Cyndia Claire Roberts was born on 14 October 1952 and Deanna Margaret Roberts born on 5 November 1954. I had to be flown from Croker Island to the Old Darwin Hospital at Myilly Point for both deliveries and then returned to the island once the children were well enough.

Our youngest daughter, Wendy-Sue Roberts, was delivered at the Old Darwin Hospital on 12 March 1959 by Dr John Brotherton who had delivered Cyndia and Deanna. Dr Brotherton also delivered three of my grandchildren and remained our family doctor until he passed away.

The American Liberator

During the time we lived on Croker, I overheard Ron and some of the other boys discussing an American Liberator plane that had crash-landed at Cape Croker (which Ron overheard from Phil Adams, the Missionary Carpenter who worked the radio). They were talking about revisiting the site to see the plane. They also mentioned that there was a picture of Betty Grable painted on the side of the Liberator. I thought, 'This I've got to see.' We waited until the weekend to make the trip to the crash site. The only major obstacle on the way to the site was our needing to cross Cape Croker Creek, which was a very wide and deep. However, when we reached the creek Ron and the other men drove the truck down the shallow part of the creek and crossed it without much trouble.

At the site of the ruins of the Liberator there she was, the picture of Betty Grable on the side of the cockpit. During the Second World War, Betty Grable had been known in the American film industry as the star with the million-dollar legs. A sad feeling rushed over me as I looked around at the ruins and found the pandanus palms where three of the airmen's lives ended so tragically, thousands of miles away from their loved ones.

Ron described how the pilot had radioed to Croker Mission and then to Darwin stating advising that he hadn't enough fuel and that they needed to head to Darwin.

There was word that they must have been on some kind of mission. The pilot was asked by his base if he could go to the mission airstrip on the fuel he had. The pilot replied 'No.'

Darwin informed the pilot that two Spitfires were flying out to check the stretch of land on Cape Croker for landing which was later found to be okay. They asked the pilot to circle the area until they arrived.

The advice given to the American Liberator pilot by one of the Spitfire pilots was to keep 50 yards (about 45 metres) off the beach as there was a mound there. They were also informed of a nearby waterhole. The pilot had made an error, bringing the plane down at an angle and causing it to hit the mound and crash land. He gave orders for the crew to bail out. Two or three of them jumped out of the plane before it had landed outside the mouth of Cape Croker Creek. Some of the people who had jumped out were hanging in the mangroves, still alive. The crew were helped down by the boys.

Ron said that the worst cases were the crew members who had stayed in the plane when it crash-landed. The plane had landed on top of a waterhole and the turret or tail gunner, had jumped out. Sadly, the tail of the plane hit him and he died instantly.

The two pilots and a navigator were still alive when they were helped out of the crashed plane and laid under the pandanus palms. One of the men was an African-American. He sat and talked to them as he dug holes in the sand for the blood oozing from their injuries. Tragically, the two pilots and the navigator eventually died under the pandanus palms. The only survivor from the crash was the African-American man.

Mr Adams and some of the older boys, Ronald Roberts, Cyril Frith, Jimmy Wauchope, Jack Scrymgour, Bill Ryan and the Aboriginal boys Lazarus Lami Lami, Dick and Jumbo Yarmirr, Jack and Joe Brown were the first to the rescue.

Mr Adams radioed to the airbase in Darwin for help advising them of the crash and the fate of the crew. It was a very sad day for everyone on the mission.

On the arrival of the American Landing Ship Dock barge and its crew they set about to collect from the ruins of the plane what they needed to take back with them to their base in Darwin. The Americans wanted to give the boys an American jeep because they were grateful for their part in helping save the lives of the remaining airman. However, Mr Adams declined the offer, saying that the boys already had what they needed on the island.

Ron also told me about another incident during the War when Mr Adams contacted the RAAF Base in Darwin by pedal radio to report the sighting of two Japanese planes, and to ask for assistance. The Darwin air base sent out two Spitfires. They found one of the Japanese planes and a 'dog fight' occurred. The Spitfire pilots ended up escorting the remaining Japanese plane into Darwin. We were told later that the other plane was shot down in between Darch and Grant Islands.

Many don't know this, but Croker Island was a secret fuel base for our Australian Air Force during the war. The reason the Japanese planes were unable to land on the island was because Mr Adams told the boys not to remove the little bushes with little red fruit growing on the airstrip. They were left there deliberately to prevent the Japanese from landing.

*

In 1953 the Wards Ordinance was legislated. This meant that the government could no longer remove any child of Aboriginal descent from his/her parents without a court order, and all full-blood Aboriginal people were registered.

In October 1956 word was passed around the island that the staff wanted to meet with everyone. I stayed behind at home to care for Cyndia and Deanna while Ron went to the meeting. He said that everyone was given a deadline to leave

Croker Island as it was being given back to the traditional people.

Ron said that he still remembers seeing many people just standing around looking stunned, in disbelief after hearing the news. No one could explain how each person felt that day. We were being told to leave our home.

One of the younger ones said, 'The government is still moving us around. I don't know where to find my mother after I leave here. This island is the only place I call home. When they took me away from my land the government gave us Croker Island.'

Another replied, 'I don't know where to find my family, either, because I was taken away when I was too young to know what tribe and country I belong to. Who is going to take me back there? The government? No, I don't think so!'

When many of our people moved to Darwin from Croker Island they arrived with their belongings in a suitcase. Some slept on the beaches. Very few found close relatives. Some joined everyone else down at the Mindil Beach camping area, where the Sky City MGM Hotel Casino now stands. The camping area was designated by the Council as a transient camping area. People parked caravans, erected tents, slept in their cars and used other modes of accommodation. The camping area was where new friendships bloomed. Some of these friendships eventually destroyed some of our people because of the influence of alcohol and loneliness.

There was also a well known story around town that those working at the Darwin Hospital at Myilly Point had to swim the flooded creek to get to work. They'd hold their clothes in one arm, extended out of the water, while they used the other arm to side-stroke across the creek. Once on the bank on the other side they dried themselves, dressed and walked up the Gilruth Avenue hill to work. Not once did it cross people's minds that there may have been crocodiles in the water.

I relocated from Croker Island to Darwin with my husband Ron and our two daughters, Cyndia and Deanna, on 20 October 1956. On our arrival we moved into one of the Army's Sidney William huts out at Pee Wee Camp, East Point. We were very lucky, because the previous residents wanted to sell their furniture. Ron bought the furniture from money he'd made from buffalo shooting on the mainland. We paid ten shillings a week for rent. The area was nice and quiet and the beach was very close to our backyard. It was a paradise. Not long after arriving in Darwin Ron bought our first car, a green Chevrolet sedan.

Ron found a job as a truckie with Thomas Brown and Sons, a local trucking firm in Darwin. He worked for the company for four to five years and then went on to work for Matt Bright with the Darwin Truck Owners as a truck driver. Ron and Matt became very good friends. When Matt retired and his son took over the business, Ron thought it best to seek work elsewhere because it wouldn't be the same without the 'old man' as the boss.

He then went to work with the Department of Works and Housing in Hudson Fysh Avenue, Ludmilla and stayed on with the government for seven years. After that he had several long-term trucking jobs.

We had a good life compared with other families in Darwin. Bob and Amy Randall, also ex-residents from Croker, lived next door to us at Pee Wee Camp with their three children, Allen, Dorathea and John. They later moved into a house at 16 Queen Street, Stuart Park, which they eventually bought.

Bob and Amy helped many of our people from Croker by offering them temporary accommodation and helping them find jobs and accommodation of their own. For many years their home was like a 'drop in shelter' for Croker Islanders.

After Bob and Amy moved to Stuart Park, my best friend from Croker, Queenie Farrow, moved into the vacant hut next door to us with her de facto husband, Pancho Price. He was one of Darwin's leading bookmakers. From time to time Pancho's young daughter Chiquita stayed over with them on school holidays. She lived and was schooled on Garden Point, Melville Island. Our children became very good friends with Chiquita and this friendship lasted into adulthood. We used to call Queenie our 'Rita Hayworth'. She was a real lady and a dear friend.

A few years after our daughter Wendy's birth we were allocated a three-bedroom Northern Territory Housing Commission home at 34 Rossiter Street, Rapid Creek. Our two older children attended Nightcliff Primary School and then went on to attend Darwin High School at Bullocky Point. Wendy-Sue attended Rapid Creek Primary School and then went on to Nightcliff High School.

Ron and I separated in 1965 and were divorced in December 1976. I was employed at the Sisters Kitchen at the Old Darwin Hospital at Myilly Point.

The following year, Cyndia and Deanna started playing softball with the Wanderers Softball Club and on the off season they also played soccer and hockey with Nightcliff. Before long both Wendy and I became involved.

Three years later, in 1968, I met Sid Gebert. We stayed together for twenty-one years, until his untimely death in 1989, when, sadly, his life ended in a road accident near Noonamah.

I was introduced to Rugby League in 1968 by Sid. He'd joined a club called Nightcliff Dragons. Ever since that year I've been a long-time supporter of the Dragons — that's some twenty-eight years of barracking. My three grandsons all played at some stage with our rugby club, with the eldest Robert now playing in the 'A' Grade. Some of the club's stalwarts are still around. People like Ron and Judy Gatley, Stem and Jackie Edwards, Rocky and Margaret Magnoli, Doug McLaughlin and wife Lyn, Rayo Adams, and Freddie 'Langlands' May. Every club has its characters and 'Langlands' was ours back in the early stages of my involvement with the club. Freddie still remains a strong supporter of the club but with age he has mellowed just a bit. Supporters like David Baxter alias 'Bust 'em up Dragons' and Norm Hoffman have now taken up the gauntlet as being the 'driving voices' in the 1990s. Kenny Storer, nicknamed 'Moose', wrote our club's sporting anthem, 'We're the Dragons'. Win or lose, the players sang it to the tune of 'Old Clementine'! It showed the great spirit our players had and still have to this day.

In 1970 Anne Pollock, Cyndia and Deanna entered their own softball club into the Darwin Softball Association's competition. They called the club 'Nightcliff Softball'. They approached me to join them, and since then I've been involved with softball. Sid was the Club's first President and he also helped with coaching for a few years. I'd like to thank these people for being by my side to keep the Dragons going through the years. My daughters, Cyndia, Deanna, Wendy, Eileen Cummings, Raymond Cummings, Stephanie Motlop, Viv King, Christine Dedman, and grand daughter Isadora.

My happiest moment in softball was in 1988 when Bob Bicknell coached Nightcliff 'A' Grade in the Northern Territory North Australian Championships. We played South Darwin. Nightcliff won 5–4 and after that year in the Darwin Women's Softball Association competition we played South Darwin again in the Grand Final and lost to them 6–5.

Cyclone Tracy, 1974

As an electrician, Sid took on contract work on communities from time to time. Prior to Christmas 1974 he had to go to Roper River to wire a large shed and the newly built houses in the community. Cyclone Tracy struck on Christmas Eve 1974, while he was away. Like all the other young people at that time of the year, my two eldest daughters Cyndia and Deanna went out to celebrate Christmas Eve with a few friends at the Berrimah Hotel, at the time a very popular nightspot in Darwin. Wendy-Sue and I babysat Cyndia's daughter, Candice, who was only two-years-old at the time, and Deanna's two children, three-year-old Isadora and two-year-old Robert.

I had the radio going on all through the afternoon and evening, listening in for the updates on the cyclone. Frequent warnings were given for people to fill up bathtubs with water and to remove everything from the walls. Wendy helped me fill bottles of water and put them in the fridge. We also boiled water and filled our thermos flask to be able to make a cup of tea later, after the cyclone. The children slept peacefully as we hurried around the house getting ready.

Wendy-Sue was only sixteen at the time and she coped very well with everything happening around us. Given her youth, I was really proud of my daughter. Cyndia was the first to arrive home in her little blue Volkswagon beetle. She came upstairs and stood in the doorway, looking at us preparing for the cyclone. She was quite tipsy from her night out and couldn't understand what all the fuss was about.

Queenie Farrar (deceased) and Ruby Braun feeding the chickens and collecting the eggs at the Croker Island mission.

The children from the Croker Island mission collecting mussels at Japanese Creek, to cook up and eat on the beach, 1949.

The Telegraph Station waterhole where I learnt to swim: 'The older girls pushed us in and we had to dog paddle as fast as we could'. (My grand-daughter Isadora Claire Roberts, is standing behind the memorial.)

An old abandoned hut at Wolfram Mine, Hatches Creek, 1989.

Kurundi Bill's house at Alipuron Outstation, Hatches Creek, 1996.

My aunt Jemima Wickham Foster Napangarti standing on the spot at Hatches Creek, where I was taken from by the police and the black tracker, 1996.

Me and my late brother, Murphy Japanangka at Uthala, Hatches Creek, Northern Territory, 1996.

Meeting my brother Pilot Carr and his family for the first time at Ali Curung in 1989. My brother and I share photographs, while his wife Trixie (back to camera) looks on with Jacki (left), and Raylene (right).

Standing at the remains of my father's grave with my brother Murphy Japanangka at Hatches Creek, 1996.

My aunty, Lena Dixon, making bush medicine as grand-daughter Jacinta Joyce Dixon looks on.

Hatches Creek Police Station now in ruins, Hatches Creek, 1989.

My uncle Stanley Holmes (left) and Sidney Gebert, my partner of 22 years, (deceased) standing outside the ruins of Lou Bailey's unfinished shop at Wolfram Mines, Hatches Creek, 1989.

My brother Murphy Japanangka and his wife Margret Napangarri standing outside Kurundi Bill's house, 1996.

Me and my brother Pilot Carr outside his house at Ali Curung, 1996.

Me (seated) in my garden with my daughters: (left to right) Cyndia Henty-Roberts, Wendy Sue Patzwald, Deanna Hodgins Roberts, Darwin 1998.

Cyndia Henty-Roberts (seated) with her daughter Csenta Roberts and her two grandsons, Tyson Rundle and Keinan Pethybridge (seated). My garden, 1998.

[From left] Stan John and Wendy Sue Patzwald (parents of Sarah and Leroy), with me and Sydney Roy Gebert at Beswick Community, 1985. Sarah Claire and Leroy John Patzwald in Tae Kwon Do gear, Darwin, 2000.

In my garden (1998). I'm seated with my great grandson Jayden Hodgins (Robert's son) on my lap. Back: Isadora Roberts, Christian Hodgins, Allen Ronald Hodgins, Robert Hodgins, and my daughter Deanna Roberts-Hodgins.

My family: (back, left to right) Candice Pethybridge holding her son, Jason, Cyndia Henty-Roberts and Chrystal Roberts; on the sofa (left to right) is Chynna Puckeridge and Tyson Lee Rundle holding his sister Raven Russell; on the floor are Csenta Roberts and her daughter Jade Devery.

My great granddaughter, Kateea Clara Hodgins, 2004.

My grandson, Christian Allen Hodgins, with his partner Bunroth Thong, 2004.

She told us she thought the house would stand the impact and with this she fell asleep with Candice on the couch in the living room.

My grandson Robert woke up first at approximately two o'clock on Christmas morning. He looked up and noticed our ceiling lifting and said, 'Nana, like Poppa Sid's boat!' I never did ask Robert what he meant by this, because he was only two at the time. Maybe it reminded him of the swaying of Sid's boat in the water. Sid used to work on the Post Master General's boat. The *Charles Todd* ferried PMG workers from Darwin to Mandorah for the day to work in the Telecommunications Section. It then returned them to the Darwin wharf in the afternoon. When we picked up Sid from the wharf the grandchildren would come along for the ride and Sid used to let them on the boat while he was packing up.

To keep Robert's mind off the noise outside, Wendy was singing 'Three Little Fish and Mummy Fish Too'. I pointed to the ceiling for Wendy to notice that the ceiling was lifting worse than before. It was now three o'clock in the morning. I decided we should go down to our station wagon which was parked under the house. I didn't think it would be safe in the house if the roof flew off. Then there was an almighty loud sound, as though a bulldozer was travelling down our street in the pouring rain. I tried to make out what the sound belonged to and where it was coming from.

The children were awake by now. Cyndia was another matter. Wendy and I couldn't wake her. I thought maybe if I raised my voice it would help, 'Cyndia wake up the cyclone is getting worse, wake up! We've got to take the children down to the car!' It never crossed my mind that we wouldn't be safe down there. Cyndia finally woke up and we headed to the outside porch with the children. I had Isadora in my arms with a blanket wrapped around her. I just had the feeling that we would be safer downstairs in the station wagon. Cyndia disagreed. She felt that it would be safer for us upstairs.

I headed down the stairs with Wendy and the children. There at the bottom of the stairs stood a family friend, Gunther Ryder. He was a godsend. Gunther was a school-teacher at Rapid Creek Primary School and had moved into Frank and Charmaine Coleman's house next door. He was house-minding while they were on holidays. Gunther had planned to fly to Singapore on the Sunday, but had postponed his holiday because of the cyclone.

He was soaking wet from the storm, dressed in a pair of shorts and with a metal hardhat on his head. He stood as brave as life, standing in a pool of blood at the bottom of the stairs. He'd cut his foot on a piece of glass, but he seemed undeterred. Gunther was more concerned about our welfare.

He said, 'Sid asked me to keep an eye on you, just in case you needed any help.' Gunther helped us to Don and Nell Davies' house across the road until the weather cleared and winds settled down.

The cyclone was like a raging enemy, destroying everything in its path. The wind was so strong that it even tried to snatch the children from our arms, as we stepped cautiously through the rain and the debris, but the children hung on tightly.

Rossiter Street was littered with hanging power lines and corrugated sheets of iron. Branches of trees and lengths of timber were strewn everywhere. It was also very dark. Someone in our group had a torch, and shone it in front of us, so that we could at least see what was ahead. The street looked like a creek in flood. Debris was still flying through the air and we were very lucky that we were not struck by any of it. I believed at the time that a guardian angel was looking over us all. On arrival at Don and Nell's home we were warned not to open the passage door because that part of the house had gone with the cyclone. Nell had a bucket in the lounge in case people needed to relieve themselves. We stayed there until daylight.

The next morning we peered out of the louvres with reservations. I expected the worst for our house and couldn't bear to look across the street. To my surprise and great relief there stood our home, 34 Rossiter Street, still in one piece, as was our station wagon under the house. However, the house next door was not so lucky. The only thing left was its foundation, the floor and the toilet. Most of neighbours' furniture had been strewn all over our lawn with other debris. My heart went out to my neighbours, Frank and Charmaine Coleman and, of course, to Gunther.

When we went over to assess the damage to our house I couldn't help but notice a picture of Christ with the words 'Bless this House'. It had been blown into our yard from next door. I looked around at our home standing strong and intact and couldn't believe that our house had been blessed in all the cyclonic rage, particularly when neighbours' homes had been demolished by the force of the cyclone.

Gunther told us the next morning that during the cyclone he had to wrap his hand in a towel to punch his way out of the Coleman's house, next door. He said he'd tried to open the front door to the house, but that the door had been shut tight from the force of the cyclone's wind. So he'd wrapped his hand in a towel and smashed some of the glass louvres in the lounge room. As a result there was a lot of broken glass on the lawn as he jumped to the ground below.

Massive evacuation

The next day we drove into the city, hoping to use the phones at the Post Office. We couldn't believe our eyes: there were long queues of people waiting to ring their families locally and interstate to let them know that they were alive and well. Boxing Day saw the beginning of the mass evacuation of more than 30 000 people. In seven days approximately 20 000 people were gathered up from their shelters and airlifted south to be met by relatives and friends. My two daughters, Cyndia and Deanna, and their children went to Adelaide to stay with friends and extended family. Cyndia and Candice were airlifted with other women and children.

Deanna, her boyfriend, Roger, and her children, Isadora and Robert, travelled by road. I tried to encourage Wendy to go with one of her sisters, but she said she'd rather stay to keep me company and wait for Poppa Sid to return. Wendy felt I'd be lonely if she didn't stay with me.

The local newspaper noted that 10 000 people drove down the Stuart Highway in their battered cars carrying the few possessions they were able to salvage from their Christmas shopping the night before. The great convoy of cars and trucks placed a burden on towns like Katherine, Tennant Creek and Alice Springs. The residents in these towns were marvellous in the way they provided assistance with food, clothing, accommodation, money, petrol and car maintenance.

Approximately three days after my daughters left, an announcement came over the radio that everyone without a job had to leave Darwin and that buses were on standby at Nightcliff High School to take people to the airport. Hazel Baban, a friend of the family, came to see me. She asked whether we'd be leaving or staying on in Darwin. I said that we'd be staying, waiting for Sid to return. Hazel then asked whether I'd be interested in registering for work as a cleaner with her at the Nightcliff High School, where the voluntary workers were staying. Wendy and I registered so we could remain in Darwin. We were very lucky and were asked to begin work the next morning.

Truckloads of workers went off to work each morning. The workers had different streets and yards to clean, as well as carting rubbish to the tip. There were other trucks of workers who worked on the rooftops. The weather was very hot and to keep their minds off the heat the linesmen and carpenters played their radios.

At the time the only people allowed by the government to return to Darwin were tradesmen. I immediately applied for Sid's return from Roper River on the basis that he was an electrician. Our application was approved.

During the first weeks after the cyclone, Darwin was like a dead town from a western movie. It was so quiet it felt like we were the only ones in town. To make matters worse the trees were bare of their leaves and there were no birds around. Hazel invited us to go and stay with her at her friend's place at Milner. Naturally we had to do a lot of scrubbing and cleaning with Phenyl and Pine-O-Clean. Hazel also invited Gunther to stay with us because he had nowhere to stay. His leg was still in plaster and he walked with the aid of crutches. We took a few days to clean the house because we had to scrub the walls, cupboards and the floors which had been covered with mildew and fungi left after the cyclone. We also gave the yard a going-over by clearing the rubble, trimming the shrubs and mowing the lawn.

We all helped to cook the meals, so there was always a variety of food on the table. Some days it looked like that a team of chefs had prepared our meals.

The day Sid arrived back in Darwin he was very quiet as we drove from the airport to our house. On the way he asked what our house looked like after the cyclone. We said, 'You'll see'. He was speechless as he looked at all the damaged houses along the way, the recently cleared blocks of lands where houses had previously stood and the naked trees that were now bared of their leaves. He shook his head in disbelief.

As we drove into our yard there was a shocked look on Sid's face. He couldn't believe that our home was still standing strong with only minor damage to the outside wall structure. He kept walking around the yard and then went upstairs to check the inside and came down again still very quiet.

Sid checked all the electrical wiring throughout the house until he was satisfied. He couldn't believe that even the wiring was okay. As we checked downstairs we found that our party lights and fridge were still in good condition, so we decided to have a barbecue and invited the voluntary workers. Darwin at this time was too lonely and depressing a place for anyone to be on their own. Word got around that we were holding a 'barbie'. People all over town asked, 'Where's the party going to be held?' The answer would come back, 'Sid and Claire's'. Others would reply, 'Just check in Rossiter Street and look for the party lights on Saturday night.'

During the night of the barbie our household generator stopped now and then because it had run out of petrol. The lights went out and everyone would be in darkness, but that didn't deter anyone from having fun. People laughed, drank and ate. Someone would call out in the dark, 'Where's the torch?' Another would answer, 'Here', 'Here'. Then another voice would call out, 'Bring the petrol'. Someone would answer, 'Coming, coming'. The men would fill the generator with petrol and start the motor.

Everyone would scream out 'Hooray!' as the power came on and the party would be in full swing again. Everyone enjoyed themselves and as they left for home they'd call out, 'See you next Saturday'. We even had the honour of Dawn Lawrie's company at our parties. Dawn was a Member of the Legislative Council and the local Member for Nightcliff. Later, she was the Commissioner of the Anti-Discrimination Commission in Darwin.

The voluntary workers had the weekends as their days off. They were always eager to see the sights of Darwin left standing. I remember one particular party when some of the locals and the voluntary workers talked about going 'geese shooting' the next morning. The men decided the voluntary workers should sleep downstairs in our old caravan so the locals could pick them up early the next morning. This was one way of ensuring the group stayed together, and avoided the locals having to drive all over town to pick them up in the morning. The next morning when they went to the caravan to wake everyone for the trip, Sid and the locals were in fits of laughter. The volunteer workers had been literally stuffed into our caravan like a 'tin of sardines'. One of the workers asked with a chuckle whether he was respectable as he was sleeping. Someone replied, 'you were too drunk to do otherwise'. There was much laughter that morning and all over town for weeks.

Our parties took away the loneliness for the volunteer workers who were so far from their interstate families. The workers also described the sadness and pain that they felt when finding bodies during the clean-ups. The hospitality that we extended in our parties was our way of showing our gratitude for their help in restoring our city.

Some of them said they'd love to tour Darwin as they hadn't seen the place. We offered our cars but warned the boys to return before dark as some cars were without headlights.

Some of the locals' cars had run out of registration and others had been damaged. The locals would say, 'That's okay mate, there's no motor registry office. Tracy took it with her, go and enjoy yourself, see the sights of Darwin and good luck.' So the cars were borrowed and returned at the end of the day. In the first two weeks or so the police were preoccupied with the clean-ups and restoring their stations, so the workers enjoyed themselves.

Women were asked not to walk the streets on their own, especially after dark because the streets were unsafe. The ratio of men outnumbered the women in Darwin at the time.

Two months after the cyclone many of the Darwin families who were interstate were getting restless and wanting to return home. However, the Building Board didn't want people returning until more homes were ready. I was told that my granddaughter Isadora was flying home with Dolly and Alfred Croker and I was asked to pick her up at the airport. Isadora kept on telling her mum Deanna, 'I want to go home to Nana. Her home blown away. Nana's got no home.'

Isadora eventually got her way and was happy to be home with me. Cyndia and Candice returned not long after and so did Deanna and Robert. Both families pulled caravans in our yard. These were supplied by the government until people were allocated their homes by the Northern Territory Housing Commission, or while their privately owned homes were restored to a liveable state.

The people who stayed behind and worked were given rest-and-recreation leave in any capital city in Australia. I really welcomed it. Sid went home to Jeparit in western Victoria to visit his family while I decided to take Wendy and Isadora on a round-Australia trip to Brisbane, Sydney and Adelaide. This was with Tom and Hazel Baban and their three daughters, Chandra, Theresa and Leslie. We visited some of our friends and we were all happy to see each other again. While visiting the cities we looked for restaurants which were selling curry and rice. It was on the last leg of our trip in Adelaide at the

'Golden Dragon' that we found curry and rice like the Chinese cooked in Darwin. The other thing we missed also was Darwin's famous Paul's Iced Coffee.

Meeting my family for the first time

On 27 September 1989 Sid and I travelled to meet my family at Ali Curung and Hatches Creek. This would be the very first time since I'd been separated from them as a child. I thank my beloved Sid for encouraging me to make that trip. He was so excited because he hadn't been that far down the track, with the exception of working at Katherine, Beswick, Hooker Creek and Milikapiti. We were fortunate that one of Sid's friends, Allen Crib nicknamed 'Cribby', lent us his four-wheel drive to make the trip. I'll never forget it for the rest of my life.

I said to myself, 'Claire, you are the prodigal daughter going home to find your mother and family.' I contacted the Community Council a few weeks before leaving, to inform them of the purpose of my intended trip. I sought their consent to conduct interviews and research at a later date. The Council approved my request to visit the community and told me they'd pass on the message to my family.

As we drove along the Stuart Highway I wondered whether I looked anything like my mother, or if any of her family looked like me.

On 29 September 1989 we drove into Ali Curung, looking for the Community Council's office to advise them of our arrival. I was apprehensive at first, wondering whether my family really wanted to see me or whether they'd think that I was forcing myself on them. We made contact with one of the Council members and went on to the community school to find Valda Shannon. Valda taught at the school and was well known to me through our playing days with our softball club. We were pleased to see each other.

Valda asked someone at the school to go and tell my family that I'd arrived. Then we walked to Valda's home, next door to my family's house.

My family made their way over to Valda's home slowly, and others followed. I introduced myself as Clara Henty and told them that my mother's name was Ruby. They nodded, saying that they knew who I was. I mentioned that my father was Harry Henty. Nita Holmes, who was helping interpret for me at the time, told me they knew who my father was. She told me they said ''Enry Endy, him proper cruel and cheeky one'. I thought 'Oops', and wondered if I should have mentioned Harry's name. I was also told that my mother had died some years previously. I was saddened by this, for it was my mother I really wanted to see after all these years.

That day I met my two grandmothers, Maudie Holmes and Georgina Wickham. I also met Stanley Holmes. Stanley was married to my niece Sally Carr (my brother, Pilot Carr's daughter). He told me he was my uncle and that I was to call him uncle. As we all greeted each other Sid made himself useful by taking photographs. He was looking to see if I looked like anyone of my family, or if anyone resembled me. I was so happy to meet my family, but was I still thinking about my mother. I asked Nita if I could see where my mother was buried. She said that someone would take me when they had a car available, because my mother's grave was at Murray Downs. The visit ended and I left my family with the hope of returning to make the trip to see my mother's grave on my next visit.

That first meeting with my family was not one where we hugged and kissed each other with the joy of not having seen each other for what seemed like a lifetime. It was more an occasion of meeting a stranger for the first time. There was no family bonding but I hadn't expected it to be any different. It was just so good to start the healing and bonding process.

Since that first meeting, many of the family have phoned me. On one occasion my brother Pilot Carr, (I'd missed him on the first trip) said, 'It was good talking to you sister, but I would now like to see you in person to talk properly to you. You know.' I agreed with him.

My friend, Eileen Cummings, who makes numerous bush trips as part of her work, told me later that the day I visited Hatches Creek, my family had told everyone around Tennant Creek that I had gone home to visit them. She said that they were really happy. At long last they had set eyes on 'their Clara' who they had lost a long time ago. Some had even thought I was dead. Spending time with my family showed me how much I'd missed out by not learning about my culture. I remembered back to the times growing up on Croker Island when I would silently think about my family. I knew in my heart then that the time would come when I would return to find my family.

The search for a sense of belonging was always a strength within me. It wasn't until I started work as the Co-ordinator at the Darwin Aboriginal and Islander Women Shelter (DAIWS) in November 1990 that I really became interested in finding out more about my mother and relatives.

I always believed that my time there was always meant to be. It was there that I met more of my mother's relatives. It was fate. At different times relatives would seek refuge at the shelter, and although they had troubled times it turned out to be a blessing for us all. Finding out that we were related made their stay at the shelter less stressful, even though they were so far from their homelands and families during difficult times. For me, it was a strengthening of my family bonds, and a sense of belonging.

During the same time, I met Shirley Lewis through our softball club. One evening after work I called into Shirley's home to see her about a softball matter. That evening I met her aunty, a dear lovely lady called Lena Nangala Dixon.

Lena asked a little about my background. As I told her my name and my country she couldn't believe her ears. She told me then that she had known my mother and that they had been very good friends. She also told me to call her 'Aunty Lena', and that she would tell me as much as she could about my mother.

I learned a lot about my mother and my family from Aunty Lena. I am ever so grateful to her for sharing her memories with me.

She remembered how most of the mothers around our community who had half-caste children and babies taken away used to talk about their children saying, 'Might be my girl or boy turn like white one now and don't want us black one no more'. Also how some women, like my mother, died before seeing their children, taking the heartache with them. I had often thought about seeing my mother, and she, me. The saddest thing for me is that I will never have a picture of my mother in my mind, nor have a reminder of her.

It was Aunty Lena who suggested I contact Murphy Japanangka, Dick Riley Japanangka and Kurundi Billy to help me research information relating to my birth, childhood, and parents. She said that it was important for me to talk to them before they passed away — because they knew my family and my mother, and father, Harry Henty.

I was fortunate too in meeting another relative, Eileen Bonney, not long after having met Aunty Lena. It was Eileen who told me that our mothers were always warned by other groups when the police or protectors were on their round-up of half-caste children. She told me our mothers usually ran away with us, or painted us black. My mother painted me black quite often so that I would look like the other children in the camps.

My brother Murphy Japanangka told me the women would collect *Banksia spinulosa* bark from the trees and burn the bark. They would leave the ashes of the bark to cool, then crush them into powder. The powder was then mixed with bullock fat into a black oily substance and this was then rubbed onto our skins. Our mothers also used the coals from the campfires as a quick method, but it wasn't as long-lasting as the oil.

Many of my family remembered the time after I was taken. They said my mother cried for a very long time. That at times she would cry out, 'They take my Clara away'. They described her grief as, 'aching with a heavy pain in her heart'. A pain that only a mother who had her children taken away from her could understand. She always hoped that I would be given back to her, but it didn't happen and she eventually died with the grief of not seeing me again.

A few years ago a friend of mine said to me, 'But look at the education you received'. I replied, 'Yes I received an education, but I also lost my mother. How would you have felt if your child or children were taken away from you and you didn't have a say?' This left my friend speechless, because she also had children.

The reunion

Between 3 to 6 October 1994 I attended the 'Going Home' Conference held at Kormilda College in Darwin.

The purpose of the conference was to raise awareness of and encourage debate about our hidden histories. The issues discussed at the conference included access to our histories, compensation, rights to land, social justice and the recognition of the displacement of many Aboriginal families in the Northern Territory. To attend was a godsend for me for this was where I would find my long-lost brother, after sixty years of looking for him.

I met Lorna Singh on the second day of the conference. Lorna was married to a man from Croker Island, Dick Tennant. Lorna asked whether I would mind grouping Dick's Stolen Generation Claim Form with the other applications from Croker Island people. She told me that Dick had attended the conference the day before but wasn't able to attend that day. When we were children on Croker Island I'd always had suspicions that Dick was my brother. I'd even asked him once. At the time Dick said that he didn't know. I took this opportunity to ask Lorna whether she knew the name of Dick's mother. She told me Dick's mother's name was Ruby and that she was from Hatches Creek. I said, 'Well then, he's my brother. I knew he was.' Lorna reinforced my thoughts. She said that Dick had always thought that I was his sister, but that he was too shy to approach me, and because he thought I was too posh to talk to.

I told Lorna that I wasn't any different from Dick and that I'd wished that he had approached me. I asked Lorna whether she would mind letting Dick know that I would phone him the next day. I felt a great sadness in my heart as Lorna left. I thought about how the years had gone by without Dick approaching me with his suspicions of our being related.

The next day I phoned Dick to make that first contact. I said 'Hello brother, this is your sister Claire. I'm sorry that I didn't see you at the conference, but never mind, we can carry on from here.' Dick gave a chuckle on the other end of the phone. It was so good to hear him laugh. He, too, was pleased to hear from me. I promised to forward him information from my research about our family at Hatches Creek and Ali Curung. I also told him that if he ever came into Darwin to give me a ring, and that he could stay at my home.

The feelings that day after finally finding my brother can't really be described. But it was a mixture of great happiness, relief, and the sense of burden being lifted from my heart. The pain I'd felt for all those years had gone.

The lost childhood years

I made my second trip to Hatches Creek on 3 December 1996 with my researcher, Mr David Alexander. I thank Roslyn Fraser from the National Australian Research Unit (NARU) for recommending him. The fact that David was well known by the local Aboriginal people in Tennant Creek, Ali Curung and Hatches Creek, made the field trip much easier.

I was really pleased to meet my skin brothers Murphy Japanangka, and Dick Riley Japanangka, Murphy's wife Margaret Murphy Napangarri (who is also my aunty), and another aunty, Jemima Wickham Foster Napangarti.

Murphy, Dick and my aunties Jemima and Margaret agreed to help me with both the oral history part of the research and by accompanying me to all the historical places of significance, especially the areas where I grew up with my mother and father as well as the place my father was fatally shot and buried.

Our first stopover was at a small place called Alipuron Outstation near Hatches Creek. One of my relatives, Kurundi Bill, (whom I had not the opportunity of meeting) was kind enough to allow us to stay overnight at his house during our stayover. Once we had settled in and finished eating we all sat outside on the verandah. David busied himself with lighting the campfire to boil the water for tea. The rest of us sat about talking.

I took this opportunity to ask Dick whether he remembered how old I was when I was taken away by the police. He said that I wasn't 'all that big' and that he was a bit older than me at the time.

Murphy maintained that the day we were taken Constable Croud knew where we were camped. That until then, no policeman had *ever* been to Wolfram Hill Mine. He said it was as though Constable Croud's trip to the area was made with the specific purpose of taking us (me, his brother Jimmy Dunno and my brother, Dick) from our mothers. Our poor mothers had no rights in those days and it was policies such as Section 6 of the *Aboriginals Ordinance 1918–1947* that took away their rights as parents.

Section 6 gave the Director of Native Affairs and his appointed delegates such as police and welfare officers unlimited powers to remove half-caste from their mothers.

The possibilities of these people finding children in communities like Wolfram Hill Mine was small. This is because our births weren't usually registered. Aboriginal mothers would take their children bush as my mother did, after the death of my father. This meant that the police would have had to travel long distances in remote and difficult country.

Murphy reported that Constable Croud had been accompanied by two Aboriginal trackers, Sandy Cameron a Kadatj, and a Luritja man called Archie. He said that they came right up to the camp and grabbed Dick, Jimmy and me and put us on the back of an old ute.

He said that we were all excited as we were lifted onto the back of the policeman's car. He remembered how we all thought that Constable Croud was just taking us for a ride. Murphy said he stood and watched us as the vehicle headed in the direction of the police station. He waited with our mothers. They waited and waited for us that day, but we never returned.

He told how he'd cried that day as he dragged branches over the ground to cover the tracks where we'd played. Our mothers were also crying. He said that the police never explained to anyone or to our mothers what had happened to us.

Eventually, Sandy Cameron, one of the trackers returned to their camp. He told Murphy's mother that we'd been taken to the Bungalow in Alice Springs. Murphy's mother then told my mother. He said that both mothers cried for many days after we were taken away. Before too long our families moved away from the camp because 'like sorry way' there were too many sad memories. Murphy described it as 'just like somebody passed away', just like we had died.

Some days later Murphy, his mother and some of the other family members started to walk to Alice Springs, intending to go to the Bungalow to see that we were alright. They walked and got lifts along the way with a couple of the miners, old Jack Higgins and his German mates Ted and Cecil. They eventually reached the Alice Springs township and walked to the Bungalow. There they hid in the hills overlooking the compound. They hid there for days, hoping to catch a glimpse of us playing around at the Bungalow, but for some reason they couldn't see any children at all. After many days of waiting, they decided to trek back to Hatches Creek through the bush tracks.

Murphy said that my mother didn't go with them to the Bungalow and that she had left her family as soon as the authorities took me and Dickie. He thought she may have returned to one of the stations, maybe Elkedra, Kurundi, Murray Downs or even Hatches Creek, but he wasn't sure. She just disappeared. As he looked at me, Murphy said, 'To your mother you were dead, you were no more, you know.'

The next morning we drove to Wolfram Hill Mine. It was here that Murphy showed me the exact location that I'd been playing with the other children on that fateful day as our mothers sat watching us. I followed him as he walked around the location, as he recalled those past events. He remembered how happy we all were that day as we ran after each other laughing and playing around the camp. He stood and pointed up to the top of the Wolfram Hill to show me the remains of the old Wolfram Hill Mine where his father and uncles had worked during the 1920s and 1930s. His eyes were as sharp as ever. I looked at every detail of the landscape before I could see the mine shaft at all.

Murphy and Jemima told how our relatives laboured for long hours in the mines. They said payment for their labour in those days was rations of flour, tea and sugar, and once in a while they would be given small portions of meat when the bosses shot a killer (bull). Murphy and Dick said that 'our' people had it real bad in those days.

Murphy also talked about a big old tree that stood strong in the area. He said that it had sheltered many a drinking day for the people of the district.

Remnant old bottles of those days remained scattered in the dirt still, but the tree he spoke fondly of had disappeared into the landscape.

I never thought I'd ever have the chance to return to my country — where I grew up as a child. The feeling in my heart that day was almost indescribable. As I stood looking around me I tried hard to picture how it would have been in those earlier days.

That same day we travelled to Kangaroo Water Hole where the police station once stood. I was surprised to see that some of the foundations of the walls were still standing. I scratched part of a wall to see what it had been made of. I wasn't surprised to find that the material included the soil from the anthills, stones and water. The ruins were in remarkable shape, having lasted all these years.

Next door to the police station were two cement blocks with steel rings affixed to the centre of the cement floor. In

1989 my uncle, Stanley Holmes, had pointed these out to me and told me how the police would chain their prisoners, especially Aboriginal and Chinese people, for long hours, sometimes for days. There were no remains to show that there'd been wall foundations or thatched roofing to cover the cement blocks.

I spent a good deal of time looking around Kangaroo Water Hole while the others sat in the car waiting for me. The elders were pretty tired by now and this was the last leg of the trip for the day before we set camp.

The final leg of our trip was to Uthala and Hatches Creek. Uthala was where I had lived with both my parents. Dick recalled how he'd first set eyes on me at Elkedra Station. He said that I was only a 'fresh baby' little girl, with my mother, Ruby. He said that my mother had gone bush to give birth to me and had returned to the station when he arrived. Bill Riley was the boss of Elkedra Station at the time.

He said that he'd seen me another time at Uthala, running through my father's house. He said he was a few years older than me and that I was the first young child to live in my father's house. He didn't say too much about my father except that he was a cruel man who did not treat his workers well.

He remembered the times he witnessed some of the Aboriginal men stealing from my father's store. He told me how one of the men would lift another over the top of the timber ledge into the shed where the dry goods were stored. The man in the shed would hand over flour and sometimes tea and sugar to the others waiting outside. The men would often do this when my father was away because they were starving.

Anyway, on one particular day Dick told how my father returned on horseback to Uthala unexpectedly. Some of the men had just finished eating damper made from stolen flour. They took off and hid; others ran as fast as they could to reach the hills. Dick said he saw my father chase one of the men on horseback until he caught him. He tied the man up with a wagon wheel chain around his neck and brought him back to Uthala. They tied the man to a tree and gave him a good flogging for stealing. Dick told me how life was really hard in those days and how the men who worked for my father had a really rough time. They were treated terribly and paid with very few rations to last a week. The only reason they stole from my father was because they were hungry. Dick wouldn't divulge the name of the man who stole the food because he'd passed away. However, he did say that the man was a Kumarra man.

Another incident was when one of the Aboriginal workers speared a bullock without my father's consent or knowledge. Dick said that my father found out what he'd done and went looking for the man. The man tried to run and hide, but my father caught up with him as he was running and cracked him with a whip, then tied him up and belted him until he couldn't walk. Murphy described my father 'as proper cruel man'.

Dick said that at the time of my father's death my mother and I were at Uthala. When word got back to her about my father's death she tried to kill herself, 'sorry way' because she had lost her 'husband' and was grieving. He said that the Aboriginal people in the area called him her husband because she had lived with him for a while and had his children.

Dick recalled that my mother packed what she could and left Uthala with me to go and stay with family at Sandy Creek.

He said that he still remembers the day my father was shot. Jack Spratt, a half-caste stockman who was my father's main stockman, was with my father at the time of his death. Seeing my father shot, he bolted on his horse to get help. Willaberta Jack had run out of the house and taken a shot at Jack Spratt. Dick said Jack Spratt was lucky because his horse went down the hill and the bullet passed over his head. Spratt rode back to the station for help and before too long a group of riders set out to find Willaberta.

My father was buried at Hatches Creek by Don Campbell, who was the Special Magistrate at the time.

Aunty Jemima said that my mother made her feel very sad, because after my father's death my mother travelled with me everywhere, she just kept travelling about from place to place. She believed that after the police took me my mother left the area, returning to live at Kurundi Station. It was here that she met up with Darby Carr and they had a son, my brother Pilot Carr. When Pilot's father returned to Yuendemu she met up with and married Albert Murphy Jabali and they went to live at Elkedra Station. Albert didn't stay long with my mother before he left her for another woman. My mother then just drifted between Epenarra, Kurundi, Elkedra, Murray Downs and Tennant Creek. She really didn't stay too long in one place.

Murphy also mentioned how he had met up with my father's brother, Walter Henty. Approximately three to four months after he'd returned from looking for me at the Bungalow he went out to live with relations at a place called Bull Creek. It was here that he met my father's younger brother, Walter Henty. Walter had arrived at the camp with a spare horse and saddle, and was looking for a new worker. He offered to teach Murphy to ride the horse and gave him a job that same day. Murphy said that he worked with Walter for a long time until Frew River and Kurundi Stations were sold. He described my uncle as the 'left-handed one' and when we asked what kind of man Walter was, he said 'old Henty was a good man, proper boy no more cheeky like your father, he never say anything bad, he never swore at the people nothing, nothing. He just run up there to give you a hand. No more cheeky one. Good stockman.'

Murphy also said that he and many of the other men liked working for Walter. They worked the land very hard, mustering and branding cattle, as well as breaking in horses. He said that those times were really hard living.

He recalled that the very last time he saw Walter was when he had gone to Alice Springs on business. Murphy said it was strange because as my uncle was getting ready for the trip he didn't show in any way that he was leaving for good. Instead, he asked the men whether he could bring them back something. The men were happy and gave him a list of things. They waited and waited, but he didn't return. They weren't pleased at all. Murphy said that he never saw Walter Henty again and called him a 'f... liar'.

Murphy also remembered that not long after my uncle left, a new boss arrived at the station. He told the man that he had bought Frew River Station from Walter and that he wanted everything, plus the horses at Aparapan, to be taken to Kurundi Station. For many years later Murphy stayed working as a stockman wherever he could find work at the various stations.

I still think how strange things were on my final field trip to Hatches Creek, Kangaroo Water Hole, Wolfram Hill Mine, Uthala and Murray Downs. It was as though my mother knew that I was there.

On Wednesday 3 December 1996 we were headed back from Hatches Creek, 59 kilometres through the vast Murray Downs area. We noticed black clouds coming in from the south and there was thunder and lightning. Murphy suggested stopping to camp and have something to eat but when we arrived there was no water in the creek so he took us to another site further on. As we drove Murphy and Dick said to me, 'Maybe we disturb old man, he knows you visit him that's why this storm following us!' I answered 'Yes might be too.'

We set camp, had something to eat and settled down to sleep but Aunty Jemima and I couldn't sleep. We lay awake, keeping a watchful eye on the lightning striking further south, hoping it wouldn't get too close to us. There were still some

stars in the sky as we both drifted off to sleep. At about a
quarter to four on Thursday morning David woke us all up.
'Let's go,' he said. The storm was now over us and the rain
was falling. We were now on our way to Ali Curung to meet
my brother, Pilot Carr, for the very first time.

We found the main road flooded. It looked like a flooded
creek, with the branches from the trees hanging in the water.
I noticed the vehicle's speedo which read 40km, then 30km.
David drove very slowly. I was feeling very scared inside but I
kept my feelings to myself. I started thinking like my people,
'Did I disturb my parents' peaceful rest or were they going to
guide us through the storm?' I was in their country now and I
was feeling close to them. 'Did the spirits of my people know
that I had come to visit the area?'

The storm worsened. David wanted to pull up but Murphy
and Dick suggested, 'A little bit more and we go to Murray
Downs community'. I couldn't see an opening but the men
knew where it was. From inside the vehicle if felt like we were
in a boat out on the sea, with water everywhere around us.

Murphy directed David through the water to an area at the
Murray Downs community. We parked between the old toilets
and the water tank. This was our shelter. The community was
in darkness and every one was asleep so we all stayed in the
Land Cruiser until daylight.

Friday morning at five o'clock, before any movement in the
community, we left Murray Downs to travel to Ali Curung,
24km away. We arrived there at seven and I couldn't believe
my eyes. No rain had fallen. How strange.

We woke my brother Pilot and his family and I told him
who I was. We were both very happy to meet each other. I met
his wife Trixie and their daughter Jackie. I had already met his
other daughter, Raelene, in Darwin. While talking to my
family the dark clouds came rolling over and the rain started
falling. I found out from Pilot that our mother is buried at

Murray Downs. He wouldn't say much about her because the heavy rain forced us to leave early. We travelled through the storm to Tennant Creek. That was sure a wet 21 kilometre trip from Ali Curung to the Stuart Highway.

I experienced a great loss of words when I met my people for the first time and learnt about my mother's death. How I wished I'd travelled much earlier; to meet my mother in person — to talk to her, and get to know her. I'd always wondered where my mother was buried and I was hoping that my brother Pilot Carr would be able to tell me. I hoped that by seeing her grave I would feel her presence, and through this be able to release all the feelings that I had hung on to for all these years.

I was fortunate to be able to find out more about my mother's movements from the Aboriginal Populations Record (No. 02097) in Tennant Creek. The records confirm that my mother moved about quite a bit. She lived at Kurundi Station in 1959. Epenarra (05/04/60, 07/03/61 16th & 30/09/63); Avon Downs (24/06/66); Murray Downs (28/07/67) Tennant Creek 1971 where she lived at Blueberry Hill with Mary Curtis. At the time of her death she was living with my brother, Pilot, at Ali Curung.

I'm planning another trip to Murray Downs in the cooler weather, and this time will avoid the wet season. Now that I know where she's buried I'll visit her grave. Doing this will let me feel much happier and at peace with myself. There is so much that I would have liked to have told my mother. Hopefully, through this final pilgrimage, my mother will somehow know that I did return, to find her.